Letters to MRS. RIGHT

Letters to Mrs. Right

MORSIA E. FRANCIS

Kingston, Jamaica

First Published in Jamaica, 2018
by Pelican Publishers Limited

44 Lady Musgrave Road
Kingston 10, Jamaica, W.I.
Tel: (876) 978-8377 Fax: (876) 978-0048
Email: info@pelicanpublishers.com
Website: www.pelicanpublishers.com

© Morsia E. Francis, 2018

ISBN: 978-976-8240-76-7

All rights reserved. No part of this publication may be reproduced or transmitted in any form or by any means, electronic, mechanical, photocopying, recording or otherwise or stored in any retrieval system of any nature without the written permission
of the copyright holder or the publisher.

Unless otherwise noted, Scriptures quoted are taken from the 1769 King James Version of the Holy Bible (also known as the Authorized Version) and from the HOLY BIBLE, NEW INTERNATIONAL VERSION®. NIV®. Copyright © 1973, 1978, 1984 by International Bible Society. Used by permission of Zondervan. All rights reserved worldwide.

Cover Design by Pelican Graphics

Book Design and Layout by Pelican Graphics

I dedicate this book to my wonderful husband, who continues to amaze me with his selfless devotion, love and care. And to my children and mother for their invaluable support, encouragement and love.

Table of Contents

Introduction xi
1. Building Your Home 1
2. Success In Your Marriage 3
3. This Marriage Business 5
4. Out Of Bounds 7
5. Love Can Curdle 9
6. Called To Serve 11
7. Create Your Own 13
8. Preparing For Friction 16
9. Ditch The History 18
10. It Must Not Be Said 20
11. The Balancing Act 22
12. Learn From The Mistakes Of Others 24
13. Harmony, Stale Or Friction Zone? 26
14. The Reconciliation Zone 28
15. Validate Yourself 30
16. Two Halves Do Not Make One 32
17. Keep Your Competitive Edge 34
18. Train Him 36
19. Speak To Yourself 38
20. The Jukebox 40
21. Choose Your Battles 42
22. Watch The Criticism: Praise Ratio 44

23.	Me Time	46
24.	Half A Muffin	48
25.	Understanding, Sympathetic Or Plain Tolerant	50
26.	Prioritize Him	52
27.	It's Not Good For The Man To Be Alone	55
28.	Validate His Feelings	57
29.	Make Him Look Good	59
30.	He Did Not Marry His Mother	61
31.	When You Marry Down	63
32.	Respect Due	65
33.	Speak To The King, Not The Fool	67
34.	He Is Not Jesus	69
35.	He's No Mind Reader	71
36.	Choose To Trust	73
37.	This Business Of Sex	75
38.	No Right To Say "No"	77
39.	Sex Is Your Right Too	80
40.	Stay In The Moment	82
41.	Raising The Dead	84
42.	Sex.....The Effective Anaesthetic	86
43.	To Spoon Or Not To Spoon	88
44.	Be Nice To Be Near	90
45.	Flirt It Baby!	92
46.	That Boyish Grin	94
47.	Think Like The Other Woman	96
48.	Never Take Him for Granted	98
49.	His Cup Will Run Over	100

50.	The Time Should Fit The Crime	102
51.	Opposites Attract But May Later Repel	104
52.	He Will Disappoint, Upset, Fail You	106
53.	Watch The Jesting	108
54.	The Litmus Test	110
55.	Seek to Understand	112
56.	You Have All Of Him... Not Really	114
57.	As Is!	116
58.	Just Let Him Be!	118
59.	Dealing With Mr. Popular	120
60.	Dealing With Mr. Cool	122
61.	Just Shut Up!	124
62.	Slewfoot's Door	126
63.	Be D.I.P	128
64.	Wow Him!	130
65.	Doing I'm Sorry	133
66.	PMS is Real	135
67.	The Big 'M' Word	137
68.	Enough of the Pretense!	139
69.	He-brews	141
70.	This Matter Of Money	143
71.	Yes Dear!	145
72.	Leave You Alone. Really?	147
73.	Watch Your Report	148
74.	Refuse To Live In Bondage	150
75.	Relationship Plaque	152
76.	Tell Him!	154

77.	A Working Penis	156
78.	Build Memories	158
79.	Nip It In The Bud	160
80.	If You Stray	162
81.	The Big 'S' Word	164
82.	How Is My Wife-Ing?	167
83.	Love Him His Way	169
84.	Be Alert!	171
85.	Too Close for Comfort	173
86.	If He Strays	176
87.	Forgiveness....A Choice You Must Make	179
88.	Pray About His Temptations	181
89.	Intuition Is Not Enough	183
90.	When Worse Comes	185
91.	I Didn't Bargain For This	187
92.	Pray Him Into His Purpose	190
93.	Help Him Secure His Blessing	192
94.	Time To Go	194
95.	From Your Mother-In-Law	196
96.	From Your Children	198
97.	From Your Best Friend	200
98.	From Your Pastor	202
99.	Going Forward	204
100.	Pray Without Ceasing	206
101.	You Get to Choose	208
	Conclusion	211

Introduction ♥

In my early Christian walk, the Holy Spirit revealed to me that Satan assigns an imp to every marriage to destroy it. I found myself counselling several married couples even though I was not married.

I remember praying to the Lord to give me a husband so that my marriage counselling could be more effective. But the probability of getting a positive answer to that prayer request was very low. Why? While I consider myself a beautiful woman and wife material, I was very independent, very focused, very self-assured – in short, very confident in my own skin. Some persons even said I was name and nature. (My maiden name is Stern).

However, the Lord did send my knight in shining armour to sweep me off my feet. My husband claims it was an easy task as I had meagre feet! In April 1991, Arnie and I got married in a beautiful wedding ceremony. I remember it as if it were yesterday. I walked up the aisle to Arnie's rendition of Lou Rawls' **Forever I Do.** He met me half way up the aisle and we stood there gazing into each other's eyes as he belted out the song in his beautiful tenor.

Arnie continues to stare me in the eyes, but not to sing. Most times he says, "Babe, there's matter in your eyes!"

We have had a blessed marriage. We are happy. Arnie has been an amazing husband. He is a blessing and I am truly blessed to be his wife and life partner. Our marriage is not perfect, but I honestly believe it's the closest to perfection we could ever reach. Every now and again, I wonder if I will wake up and find that I was just dreaming. We have also been blessed with two fine sons, Jhuvon and Joel. I am eternally grateful to God for His blessings on us.

So, I am in a great marriage, but I am painfully aware that I am in the minority - even in the church. I have seen so many failed marriages. So many divorces, separations or couples just hanging on together by a thread. There is no spark. I believe it is a deliberate strategy by the enemy of our souls to tarnish a beautiful institution, which is intended to be a reflection of the relationship between Christ and the church (his bride).

The idea of **Letters to Mrs. Right** came to me a couple years ago. I wanted to share some of the principles that worked not only in my marriage, but in other marriages. I have counselled many married persons, especially wives. In a number of cases, with a little guidance and change in perspective, what was initially thought to be a big issue was reduced to a non-issue. I therefore yearned to share some of the issues that I have encountered over the years and the solutions which worked. My views are based on biblical principles as I believe that when you apply the principles of the word of God to your marriage, you have a greater chance of success.

The book consists of 101 letters written to wives in general and the Christian wife in particular. However, I am very sure that husbands will enjoy reading it as well. In fact, some wives might even think that the book is biased in favour of their husbands! **Letters to Mrs. Right** covers a number of issues including topics that may even be considered taboo. However, each letter I have been inspired to write addresses an issue which at least one person is struggling with.

The letters are short - in keeping with my height (I am five feet, half inch tall; yes - half inch!) - but hopefully the points will be grasped. I truly hope that the contents of this book will provide some guidance on how to address some issues that commonly cause problems in marriages. A number of themes are repeated throughout the letters. For example: *do not nag your husband; focus on his positives; and the prayer of a righteous person is powerful and effective.*

Despite the very disheartening statistics on marriages, I know that marriages can be beautiful. I interact with couples who are happy - very happy. And my philosophy in life is, "If one person succeeds at something, then others can too."

My prayer is that as you read the pages of this book, you will be inspired to do what it takes to ensure the success of your marriage. I pray that with the help of the Lord, you will greatly invest in your marriage and thus reap great dividends. May God bless you and may you experience fulfillment, joy and excitement in this beautiful institution called marriage.

1. Building Your Home ♥

Every wise woman buildeth her house, but the foolish plucketh it down with her hands. Proverbs 14:1

Whatever you say or do represents building materials used in the construction of your marriage. You get to decide what type of marriage structure you want and how you will contribute to the structure being built. What I am saying is simple; before you act or speak, ask yourself: *will this action or expression strengthen or weaken my marriage?*

I must hasten to add that I know there are persons who believe that it is impractical to speak to yourself when you are angry. I beg to disagree. If the perceived consequence of uncontrolled actions is great, then we will control ourselves. For example, if – or should I say - when your boss gets on your nerves, do you simply tell him or her what comes to your mind? Of course not, unless you have another job waiting. Instead, you bite your lip and control what you do or say. Why? Because you risk losing your job if you act out your feelings. The stakes are too high, so you control yourself.

Well my dear, use the same technique to control yourself when your partner gets on your nerves! Note I did not say 'if,' I said 'when.' He *will* get on your nerves. But you must control how you act and react. The stakes are too high not to.

In the same way you would not tolerate an insect infestation in your home, you should likewise not allow 'bad spirit' infestation. You must make it clear to yourself, your spouse or any other occupant of your home, that certain actions or attitudes have no place there. Shouting, disrespect, malice and fighting are some of the "bad materials" you should avoid using to build your home. You must be vigilant.

Create a vision of the type of home you want and then commit to using only 'good materials' to build it. Oprah Winfrey once said, *"Create the highest, grandest vision possible for your life, because you become what you believe."* And even if you do not become what you believe, you certainly cannot become what you do not believe! So, I encourage you to first believe that your home life can be great and then starting using only those materials that will result in a great home.

Remember the word of God in Psalm 127:1 says, *Except the Lord build the house, they labour in vain that build it.* So in all your building do not forget the Lord!

2. Success In Your Marriage ♥

Success in marriage is less about doing the big things, than it is about doing those little things, day after day…Unknown

Even in the church, the divorce rate is alarmingly high. The success of a marriage is not dependent on only one partner. But, if at least one resolves to fight everything (and everyone) who comes against the marriage, then the possibility of success is greater. The bible says in Ephesians 6:12, *For we wrestle not against flesh and blood, but against principalities, against powers, against the rulers of the darkness of this world, against spiritual wickedness in high places.* You must decide that your marriage will not be part of the negative statistic.

When I got married, I decided that the imp assigned to my marriage was going to have a hard time with me. I was going to pray every single day for my marriage. You have to be militant when it comes to the success of your marriage. The enemy must know that you will not go down without a fight. That means that you will weigh your words and deeds. You can decide whether your words or actions will contribute to the success or the destruction of your marriage. Fight for the success of your marriage. It requires deliberate actions. You may not feel to fight, but just the thought of your imp being victorious should motivate you to fight on.

You and your partner should decide how success looks and feels in your marriage; not based on someone else's. Never compare your marriage with another. You both should articulate your needs and each should resolve to meet those needs as best as possible. Marriage is a beautiful institution designed by God for two people to come together and reflect the glorious relationship Christ has with His church.

I have come to realize that one of the main factors which contributes to the success of a marriage is expressing genuine care for your partner on a daily basis. One simple act that my husband and I practise in our marriage, is to ask each other if we would like to share anything we put to our mouth to eat or drink - even if it is a glass of water. It communicates that we are always thinking about each other. We consistently care for each other. We learned early in our marriage that the little things were really the big things. Little acts of kindness and expressions of care have formed the glue in our marriage. I encourage you to develop the habit of genuinely caring for your partner on a daily basis. Romans 12:10 tells us to *Be devoted to one another in love. Honour one another above ourselves*.

3. This Marriage Business ♥

Don't be in a relationship if you are going to act single.
Sushan Sharma

Unless you are in a "business marriage," you can't do as you please. Once married, you can't expect to have the freedom to go where you want to go, when you want to go, without informing your spouse. Yes, you are your own big woman and you can very well do as you please. Of course, you can! But with that attitude it means that your spouse can do the very same. He too can do what he pleases; go where he wants at any time without any discussion or even informing you. If that is what you want, then you do not want a spouse. You want a roommate!

And even in a roommate relationship, since you share the same space, it would be courteous to inform your roommate of your going-ins and your coming- outs. That kind of sharing of information reflects a respect for each other and lends itself to a healthy and open relationship.

I know you may be saying, "Well, no one is going to control me." Here is a perspective you may not have considered. When people care for each other, they want to minimize anxiety as far as possible for the other party. So, instead of your spouse wondering where you are, if you are OK, simple communication could eliminate that anxiety. Honest, respectful, caring communication is vital to the success of any marriage.

What if he doesn't inform you of what he is doing and where he is going? Well, 1 Thessalonians 5:15 says, *Do not render evil for evil but follow that which is good*. Remember, how you treat your spouse should not be dependent on how he treats you, but on your desire to become the godly wife that God wants you to be. It is not easy at times. But if you bear in mind that you serve your spouse as unto God, your decisions will then be made in keeping with what you ought to do in spite of how you may feel.

My dear, this marriage business is serious business and you have to make it your business to take it seriously.

4. Out Of Bounds ♥

Boundaries are not meant to control others; they are meant to be used as guidelines for you to know what is acceptable and what is not in your life. Sheryl Griffin

There are certain actions and utterances that do not have any place in a marriage - they are simply out of bounds. Actions such as name calling, long malice (sometimes short breaks in communications is necessary for the partners to collect themselves), physical abuse, and disrespect, to name a few. Never speak disrespectfully of his relatives especially his mother. Even if you believe he does not like her, it is never OK to disrespect his mother. Believe me, it will touch a nerve. It is never OK to wish him evil; saying you wish he were dead! Having a public spat should also be no – no. These things have absolutely no place in marriage.

Marriage is a partnership between equals. No one should feel superior to the other and no one should be made to feel inferior. You and your partner should sit and determine where you both think the boundaries should be in your marriage. You should both agree not to cross the boundaries; and also to commit to that agreement. You should also agree what actions the aggrieved partner might take when boundaries are crossed.

It will take discipline, determination, self-control, restraint and the power of the Holy Ghost to help you not to cross the boundaries in the heat of an argument. You must develop your own method of control, which will prevent you from going out of bounds. So for example, if you are very upset, let your spouse know that you are upset and you would rather cool off before you speak. Resist the temptation to blurt out the first thing that comes to your mind.

"Speak when you are angry, and you will make the best speech you will ever regret." Laurence J.Peter.

5. Love Can Curdle ♥

Then Amnon hated her exceedingly; so that the hatred wherewith he hated her was greater than the love wherewith he had loved her.
2 Samuel 13:15

More than fifty percent of couples who get married get divorced. The once lovey-dovey, can't-get-enough-of-you couples can no longer stand the sight of each other. In fact, if they had a choice, some would not share the same planet with their former spouse. The intense hatred for each other sometimes lasts for years and for some, for the remainder of their lifetime.

Never believe it cannot happen to you. You must make a conscious decision to avoid words and actions that could damage your marriage. One such thing is not saying the first thing that comes to your mind in the heat of the moment. Bite your lip if you have to, but train yourself in that discipline. The bible says in 1 Corinthians 14:32, *The spirits of the prophets are subject to the prophets*. This therefore means that you can be in control of your words and your actions. One attribute of the Fruit of the Spirit is self-control. You need to exercise a healthy dose of self-control. Other portions are gentleness, meekness, and goodness.

I encourage you to put a mental tag: *Fragile - Handle With Care*, on your relationship. It is a decision that you must make. You must pay attention to your words and actions towards your spouse. Never take your spouse for granted to the point where you act or speak without thinking.

It can take years to build what we believe to be a loving, caring relationship and it may take just one careless word spoken in anger to destroy that relationship. I encourage you to train yourself to protect your love from turning sour!

6. Called To Serve ♥

By love, serve one another Galatians 5:13

I am convinced that the key to a successful marriage is found in Galatians 5:13, *By love serve one another*. If you are not prepared to serve your partner, then marriage may not be for you. Marriage calls for deliberate, intentional choices to make your partner happy. Will it be easy? Not all the time. Irrespective of your level of compatibility, there are areas where you are as different as night is from day. You must therefore engage the Holy Spirit to assist you to navigate through the difficult times, remembering that you are called to serve.

Service is a choice. It's not about how you feel. It's about what you can do for the greater good of your marriage. Jesus demonstrated perfectly what it means to serve. Imagine, the King of kings and Lord of lords bent down and washed the feet of his disciples. He didn't have to do it, but he wanted to demonstrate how we should serve each other.

The call to serve is an individual one. It's about serving as unto the Lord. Colossians 3:23 says, *Whatsoever ye do, do it heartily as to the Lord and not unto men*. Use challenges in your marriage as occasions to seek the Lord and ask Him how best to serve your partner that He, God, may be glorified through your actions. Yes, it will take some unnatural course of action. You will not feel like doing what God instructs you to do. In fact, you may even feel it's downright unfair. But learn this, choosing to do things His way will make your marriage stronger. You will also feel better about yourself.

Ralph Waldo Emerson says, *It is one of the most beautiful compensations of life that no man can sincerely try to help another without helping himself.*

The marital journey is one of service; though not servitude. It is important that you develop that mindset which is prepared to serve your husband "as unto the Lord." Just imagine being graded by the Lord on your service to your husband. Wouldn't it be great to hear, "Well done, thou good and faithful servant!"

7. Create Your Own ♥

Marriage is a mosaic you build with your spouse. Millions of tiny moments, that create your love story. Jennifer Smith

No two marriages are alike. Even if identical twins married identical twins, their journeys would be different! So as you say **I do**, recognise that you are beginning a new life that never existed before. It is well advised to learn the habits of successful couples as long as you are aware that you both must decide what your success will look and feel like. Never be pressured into doing it like the Jones'. A marriage is a wonderful opportunity to create something beautiful out of nothing. You do not enter a marriage. You create one. So two of you should decide what will work in your creation. There are conventional roles that each partner normally takes on, but nothing is cast in stone. Agree on what will work for both of you.

I remember one Saturday I was waiting with my two young boys for their trim in the barber shop. A young man walked in, and upon seeing me looked rather puzzled. He then came up to me and said, "You are here at the barber with your sons and I just passed your husband at the market shopping, how come?"

"How come what?" I asked.

My husband enjoys shopping at the market. He says 'it's therapeutic' (I guess he needs some therapy being married to me!) I had no problem with going to the barber with my boys. That worked for us!

It is important that you have a shared vision of what your marriage should be like and work at it. While a successful marriage requires the commitment of both persons you should at least decide how you will contribute to the reality of that vision. That contribution should then be frequently assessed for relevance and effectiveness. Remember you will both change many times throughout your life together, so you will need to constantly assess whether your contribution is still meeting the changing needs of your partner.

How will you know if your contribution is still relevant and effective?

Ask him!

You should have frequent discussions on how you feel about your marriage. This will help to strengthen the bond between you and your spouse. The discussions should be very candid. They should communicate to your partner that you are committed to pleasing him and want to do everything in your power to make him happy.

Never forget that you are creating your love story by the things you do and say to your spouse; by the way you treat him both at home and in public. How you address him and respond to him; the places you go or do not go with him. In fact, that story is impacted by every interaction with your spouse.

Be aware also, that your story is being read by those with whom you interact and even by those with whom you may never cross paths. So create a story that makes for pleasant, inspiring reading.

8. Preparing For Friction ♥

Friction is inevitable, which if not managed, could result in dis-harmony. Unknown

Friction in marriage is inevitable. No two persons will feel the same way about everything all the time. That will not happen. So prepare for friction. I have three simple rules for dealing with friction. They are: choose your battles; don't sweat the small stuff; reserve your energy for big-ticket items.

Always apply the half-full, half-empty principle. People will view the same things differently. Decide beforehand how you will deal with friction when it happens.

Note I said 'when', not 'if'. It will happen!

Another important ingredient for a successful marriage is the partners' ability to handle differences. It is a matter of choice. You must train yourself to accept that different does not mean wrong. Irrespective of how strong your views are, you must respect the views of your partner.

Set boundaries before friction starts. For example, agree beforehand that neither party will disrespect the other, irrespective of how angry you are. Proverbs 15:1 admonishes, *A soft answer turneth away wrath...* You have to practice to control your anger and don't let it control you. Anger is one letter away from danger. Protect your marriage from danger by preparing for and deciding how you will handle your friction. It takes maturity to remain calm and respectful when there is disagreement. But you must. In fact, this ability is a true reflection of your level of maturity!

It is not the compatibility of a couple that will cause them to succeed, but rather how they handle their incompatibility (paraphrased). *Diane Sollee, founder and director, Coalition for Marriage, Family and Couples Education*

9. Ditch The History ♥

Love does not keep record of wrongs. 1 Corinthians 13:5

History was not one of my favourite subjects in high school. I didn't see the relevance in learning about events that happened long before I was born. I have since come to appreciate the importance of history. It was Marcus Garvey who said, "A people without the knowledge of their past history, origin and culture is like a tree without roots."

Having said that, however, I hasten to warn you to resist the temptation to remind your spouse of all the wrongs he has done in the past every time you have an argument. Ok, so you do not remind him of all his wrongs, only the ones from the week before and the week before that...

The fact is, bringing up the past may very well weaken your position, especially if your spouse was of the opinion that those issues were resolved. So if he did something which upset you, but you talked about it; forgave him and made up; in his mind the matter is settled. He has likely thrown it in the sea of forgetfulness. Raising that issue again, is tantamount to going in a garbage heap to pick up something you had previously discarded, and using it. Your spouse might very well lose confidence in your word and decisions. This kind of situation is a haven for animosity. Your spouse may feel betrayed and upset that you have brought up issues that were previously resolved, while you will get upset that he is not trying to resolve the issue at hand.

I encourage you therefore, try to exercise great, and I mean really great self-control to focus on current issues and refrain from the history sessions.

When there is a disagreement, focus on the issue at hand. Be specific about how this action is making you feel. Resist the temptation to use extremes such as "never" or "always." These are also inflammatory words, which shift the focus from the real issue. You must remember that the enemy is present in every argument and his job is to twist what is being said so that he can destroy your marriage.

Resist the temptation of using the history of your spouse's wrong doings to destroy your marriage. Gary Chapman said, "The best thing we can do with the failures of the past is to let them be history."

10. It Must Not Be Said ♥

But fornication, and all uncleanness, or covetousness, let it not be once named among you, as becometh saints. Ephesians 5:3

The bible says in Ephesians that there are certain things which should not be named even once among us as Christians. Similarly, we should ensure that our spouse never says certain things of us. Live intentionally, live strategically, live purposefully. Develop a list of things you would not want your husband to say of you. When you do that, you will make serious effort to deliberately avoid certain things.

Remember, your list is not about your spouse and his behaviour. It is about you and your behaviour. After you have developed your list, ensure that you do not allow anyone, not even your spouse, to cause you to veer off track. It is your track, your chosen pathway. As difficult as it will get at times, as tempting as it will get at times, stay on your chosen path.

So what are some of the resolutions you could make? You could decide that you would not want your husband to say you disrespected him, you belittled him or you are a nag... You decide. Whatever is on your list, keep it mental.

You must refer to it when you are most tempted. I am not saying you will never find yourself doing what you resolved not to do, but if you exercise self-control often enough, it becomes easier.

Engage the help of the Holy Spirit to empower you to stick to your resolutions. If or when you fail, it is not enough to simply brush off the failure and say, "I'm only human." Many times as Christians we hide behind the cloak of 'being human' rather than admitting our wrongs and resolving to try our best not to repeat them.

So it's time to prepare your mental list. It may even be helpful to write it down. Having prepared your list, commit to it!

11. The Balancing Act ♥

To every thing there is a season, and a time to every purpose under the heaven Ecclesiastes 3:1

Life can be very demanding. The fact is, most times we over-commit ourselves and as such some things will get squeezed. Most often, quality time with our spouse is that thing which gets 'squeezed' in favour of the many other things we are convinced that we just have to do. However, our actions must communicate to our spouse that he is important. You must communicate that your time together is special. You cannot simply make your plans without any consideration as to how it will impact your partner. The Lord God said in Genesis 2:18, *"It is not good that the man should be alone*. He must feel that he is important to you and not just some appendage, which must be tolerated.

Be careful of the signals you send to your spouse. Do your actions say, "Hey listen, I have things to do. You had better find something to do too." Or do they say, "I am willing to change my plans to accommodate you because you are special to me?"

This balancing act can be a real challenge. Sometimes you may even have to review the amount of time you spend at church. The truth is, many wives spend more time at church than they spend with their husbands. If your husband is not a Christian or does not attend your church, you are living dangerously! You are creating an avenue for the enemy to destroy your marriage.

You must seek God's guidance and wisdom in how to achieve an appropriate balance. James 1:5 says, *If any of you lack wisdom, let him ask of God, that giveth to all men liberally.*

12. Learn From The Mistakes Of Others ♥

Learn from the mistakes of others, cause you can't live long enough to make them all yourself. Unknown

One of the things I pay keen attention to is the complaints men have about their wives. Some of the common ones are that wives are:

- ♥ Not meeting their sexual needs
- ♥ Nagging
- ♥ Controlling
- ♥ Vindictive
- ♥ Critical
- ♥ Negative
- ♥ Too Perfect
- ♥ Not maintaining their attractive appearance
- ♥ Not meeting their sexual needs (repeated for emphasis)

I have many times asked myself, "What are the complaints my husband would have about me?" In fact, at times I ask my husband if there is anything that I do that he doesn't like, or if there is anything I could do more of? As night follows day I will get the same answer; more sex!

I remember a good friend had complained to me that early in his marriage, he would try to play with his wife, but she would 'run' him, saying he played too much! He said he got turned off and gradually stopped the playing. However, later in the marriage, she wanted to play but he couldn't. He said he had dried up. He couldn't respond. Well I said (in my heart of course) thanks for telling me. Even though I was not a playful person, I would transform into one. If my husband wanted to play, then I would be his playmate. I shudder to think of him having to find someone else to play with!

Before marriage, many women will do things with and for their partner that they really do not like to do.

Once married, the pretence ceases. They can no longer be bothered to do things that do not interest them. This is a grave, very grave mistake. This usually leads to conflict, tension or a gradual growing apart.

Never forget that it is easier for your marriage to fail than succeed. So you have to make deliberate choices to prevent it from failing. Learning from the mistakes of others will greatly assist you in succeeding in your marriage.

13. Harmony, Stale, Or Friction Zone?

A wise woman recognizes when her life is out of balance and summons the courage to act to correct it. Suze Orman

I have concluded that marriage operates in one of three zones - the harmony zone, the stale zone or the friction zone. In the harmony zone, there is intimacy, deep communication, play, laughter and deep emotional connection. Needs are met. There is positive energy flowing. The relationship is rhythmic and operating like a well-oiled machine.

In the stale zone, there is civility, communication takes place only on a "need to" basis and even then it's superficial. There is no emotion. There is no passion. There is no connection. There is much tolerance.

In friction zone there is much energy - negative energy; constant confrontations, arguments, malice, even fighting. The partners can see absolutely nothing positive in each other. The focus is always on some negative issue.

The ideal situation is to operate in harmony zone at all times but that will not happen. You can, however, decide that once you realise that you are not there, you will pull out all stops to get back there. Is that easy? Of course not! But you must push through your stubborn will, put aside your pride and do your part to get back in harmony zone.

So what about the other party? After you have done all that you believe is in your power to do, you can only pray the other person back into the zone. You can't force him, you shouldn't nag him nor demand that he returns, especially if you were the offending partner. If you are the victim, I encourage you to wrestle and wrestle until you get your breakthrough blessing. You may have to return to the zone with a limp (think Jacob; Genesis 32:26), but return as quickly as possible.

In order to identify the zone that you are operating in, you must be alert and sensitive to the energy flowing between you and your spouse. You have to watch the gradual slide. While you may not be operating in the friction zone, you could be growing apart gradually until one day you both realize that you do not know each other. You must be intentional and deliberate to operate in the harmony zone. You must deliberately do and say the things that will keep you in harmony zone. For example, you could decide that you will share an intimate moment with your spouse every day.

That moment could be a simple thing as giving him a kiss, a hug or calling him just to touch base. Whatever you choose to do, make sure you do not choose to do nothing!

14. The Reconciliation Zone ♥

Emphasize reconciliation, not resolution. Rick Warren

One of my favourite subjects in school was accounts, thus I chose to become a chartered accountant. Preparing the bank reconciliation statement was one of my favourite topics. I will now give you a crash lesson on bank reconciliation statements. Why? I believe that applying the principle will save you much fuss and help maintain harmony in your home. So here goes: Let's say you have $10,000 to open a current account at the bank. You take your $10,000 to the bank and open the account. The bank gives you a cheque book. You leave the bank knowing it has $10,000 for you. The bank's record will also show that it has $10,000 for you. No problem there.

Let's say your friend asks you for a $5,000 loan and you draw her a cheque. After you give your friend the cheque, you subtract the $5,000 from the original amount of $10,000 leaving a balance of $5,000. As far as you are concerned, the bank now has $5,000 for you. Right? But say your friend got some money before she reached the bank and decided to hold on to the cheque for a week. During the week, the bank deducted $500 for bank charges. You will not know this until you receive your bank statement or check your balance. So as far as the bank is concerned, it has $9,500 for you, while your record is saying the bank has $5,000 for you. Which is the right figure? Would you say the bank? Or you? Would you say the bank's figure of $9,500 is wrong? The fact is the bank has not yet been presented with the $5,000 cheque to reduce your balance and you have not yet deducted the $500 bank charges in your records.

So the balances are different, yet neither is incorrect. It is in preparing your bank reconciliation statement that you reconcile the two balances. It is the same way you and your partner will at times see the same things differently. As such, it behoves you to develop a healthy dose of tolerance for differing views, although it is one of the hardest things for humans to do. It takes a serious, deliberate effort. It takes practice and self-control. It takes the help of the Holy Spirit.

However, it must be done if you want your marriage to succeed. You must seek to arrive at the reconciliation zone when differing views emerge, as they most definitely will!

15. Validate Yourself

Never forget to value yourself. Never seek validation outside of yourself. Debasish Mridha

The bible says in Matthew 19:19, *Love thy neighbour as thyself*. This implies that you love yourself. The bible gives us permission to love ourselves. To be vain? No! To worship yourself? No, but we must love ourselves. We must possess a strong sense of self-worth. Your self-worth must not be based on your interaction with your husband. You must recognise that you are a whole and complete person, created in the likeness and image of God for a particular purpose. The bible says in Psalms 139:14, *You are fearfully and wonderfully made*. Whether you are short, tall, fat, slim, you are fearfully and wonderfully made. You must never belittle yourself or allow yourself to be belittled. Understand that no one can rob you of your self-esteem without your permission. That permission should not be given to anyone, not even your spouse.

It therefore means that at the earliest sign of any behaviour or utterances that you deem demeaning, you should unequivocally communicate your disapproval. Never brush it aside. Never sweep it under the carpet. Do not try to rationalize. Calmly and respectfully state that you do not appreciate being treated or spoken to in that manner. Do not allow yourself to be bullied into accepting the behaviour or utterance. While you may not be able to get your spouse to see things your way, you must communicate how you feel. It's your feelings!

You must be comfortable in your own skin and not be dependent on anyone to validate you. In fact, in many cases one of the main characteristics that attracts a man to a woman is her confidence! Never go without yours, or else, you are not fully dressed!

16. Two Halves Do Not Make One ♥

You can never be happy as someone's other half unless you can be happy as a whole all on your own. Unknown

As you start your marriage, you are told the two should become one. The oneness here is a unison of purpose and vision; especially the vision of what your marriage should become. In order to have this united vision, you must have a vision for yourself. You should not leave the direction your marriage ought to take solely to your spouse. You are a complete human being. Not a half. I know you have heard persons refer to their spouse as their "other half". No, you are not a half. You are a whole person and you must recognise and appreciate that.

The bible says in Romans 8:17 that *you are heirs and joint heirs with Christ*. That means that you are just as important as your spouse. Irrespective of the differences in status, social class, economic substance or educational achievements you are someone of value. A complete human being. When God looks at you both, He sees two hearts; hearts that should have decided to come together to achieve His purpose for their lives. Two hearts that are committed to living a life which is pleasing to Him and which glorifies Him.

Marriage should provide an opportunity for each person to grow and reach full potential. Each person should feel accepted as a unique creation of God. An inferiority complex has no place in a marriage. While the bible teaches that the man is the head of the woman and she should submit to her own husband, it also teaches that we should submit one to the other. (Ephesians 5:21).

You must accept that God loves you as a unique person; a whole person. If you see yourself as anything less than that, there will be trouble in your marriage. You will either be excessively dependent on your spouse for validation or you will be excessively suspicious of your partner's every move. Either way spells trouble for the union.

17. Keep Your Competitive Edge ♥
Be ye steadfast, unmoveable. 1 Corinthians 15:58

You are not the only girl your husband could marry. Ouch! I know, I hear your ego! And even though he may whisper in your ear: *You are the only girl for me*. That's not true. You may be the only girl for him at that time and in that space. But believe me, if he lived elsewhere or waited a few more years, he would have met someone else with just as nice or even nicer qualities.

It is therefore important, in fact, very important, that you maintain the trait(s) which attracted him to you in the first place. You must be deliberate in doing the things that please your husband. It's not about what you think should please him. It's about what actually pleases him. If you are unsure, ask him. Study him. Seek to understand him. Never forget you are married to a man; a man who is aroused by sight and smell. Therefore, always make an effort to be attractive and smell good. Even when doing chores, be always mindful of your appearance.

On the other hand, your competitive edge may be something else. Maybe it's your chaste conduct or your sense of humour. Whatever it is, find out and maintain it.

Even if your husband is a pastor, bishop, apostle or holds another high office in the church, he still has male hormones. Those hormones are not baptised. They are not Christian hormones. So treat your husband as a man whose continued attraction to you is important – because it is. When the attraction goes, other things tend to follow and soon your marriage is in shambles and you cannot understand why. I urge you to do everything in your power to keep him attracted to you.

Begin by knowing your competitive edge and keep working it!

18. Train Him ♥

You teach people how to treat you by what you allow.
Stephen Covey

Your partner will never treat you perfectly all the time. The onus is on you to point out to him, at the first occurrence of a word or deed that you find offensive, that his action is unacceptable. You should make it quite clear that you were offended. Sometimes we are deeply offended by the actions of our partners and they have no clue that we are offended until we "dry up" with them. We withdraw. We malice them. And of course, we draw for our potent weapon - no sex!

That is not an acceptable course of action. When we are offended, we should say so. We should not spite him or retort in a way we know will return the offense. 1 Peter 3:9 tells us that *we should not render evil for evil, or railing for railing: but contrariwise blessing.* In any case, our goal should be at all times to operate in the harmony zone and retaliation will not advance this goal.

This, however, is not to say that we should ever settle for being treated less than equal in the relationship. You must speak up. I know you may not feel like it, but seek God's grace to help you even if you are afraid. Eleanor Roosevelt said "you can only expect what you accept". So speak up, even if your voice shakes.

While you should express to your partner your displeasure at any acts or utterances which you deem disrespectful, it is equally important that you do not communicate that displeasure in a disrespectful manner. If your partner does not change, you must decide how you will react. If you have no intention of leaving him because of the habit, then change how you react to the offense. Maya Angelou makes it simple, "If you don't like something, change it. If you can't change it, change the way you think about it."

19. Speak To Yourself ♥
Then I consulted with myself. Nehemiah 5:7

I am always talking to myself. While travelling on a bus some time ago I noticed that the person sitting beside me drew away from me. It was only then that I realised that my little conversation with myself was audible. I guess she felt that I was insane. But I still believe that people should speak to themselves.

I am by no means suggesting that you do so aloud in public. But you must develop instructions to self that you commit to follow as soon as the relevant situation arises.

For example, one of my well-used instructions to self is that nagging is off limits. So despite the urge to reiterate and re-emphasize a point, if it borders on nagging then I instruct myself to bite my lip. And I mean literally!

The bible instructs us in Ephesians 5:19 to *Speak to yourselves in psalms and hymns and spiritual songs, singing and making melody in your heart to the Lord.* That is sound advice and meant to be practiced. Speak to yourself and remind yourself what the word of God says. For example when you are tempted to say something unkind, you remind yourself of Ephesians 4:32 which says, *And be ye kind one to another, tenderhearted, forgiving one another, even as God for Christ's sake hath forgiven you.*

Will it be easy? No. But you must continue to speak to yourself until your spirit comes under subjection to the Holy Spirit.

Note that the speaking is not just a casual surface conversation... no, it should be deep conversation... you may have to argue with yourself a bit... well, more than a bit... but the objective is to reach a place in your spirit where you accept that you must do what you do not feel like doing because you know it's the right thing to do... or not to do!

It is said that speaking to oneself is a sign of insanity. Well I recently heard that not speaking to yourself is definitely insanity. You can decide!

20. The Jukebox

Knowledge isn't power until it is applied. Dale Carnegie

I grew up in an era when people used to punch jukeboxes in bars. They would put in a coin and select the song they wished to hear. As a married person you should also have a jukebox; a "jukebox of principles." Whenever you have a disturbance in your spirit, select an appropriate principle from your "jukebox" and apply it. The aim is to resolve the situation as quickly as possible and return your spirit to a peaceful state.

Look at issues from several perspectives. Sometimes you may have to select more than one principle to apply, as one may not be enough. If you arrive at a perspective that, while different from your own, is reasonable, then assume your partner holds that perspective. (Whether that is so or not!) This will ease the disturbance in your spirit. Always remember that no two human beings will always think the same way, to the same degree about every situation. It will not happen. Ensure that your principles are aligned to the word of God. Irrespective of how strongly you feel about an issue, if the principles you want to apply do not line up with the word of God, you should try your best to change those principles. There is a common expression, 'Methods may change but principles should not.'

However, if your principles go contrary to the word of God, then you should change those principles!

The Psalmist said in Psalms 119: 105: *Thy word is a lamp unto my feet and a light unto my path*. It's the word of God that should guide your actions. You have to practice to punch your principles from the jukebox of God's word.

A friend once told me that she got home from work to find her sink filled with dirty dishes even though her unemployed husband, who was not sick, was at home all day. She said her first reaction was to cuss. She felt the anger rising but then, she remembered Psalms 51: 10, which says, ...*Renew a right spirit within me*. So she asked the Lord for grace to right her spirit. She got the grace and didn't cuss. She simply looked at the dishes and went to her room. Her husband got the message. He got up and washed the dishes.

She chose to 'punch' Psalms 51: 10 from the jukebox of God's word. It's not enough to know the word of God, we must apply it.

21. Choose Your Battles ♥
The art of being wise is knowing what to overlook. William James

I have heard it said that a man wants to marry 'Miss Right' but her first name must not be "Always'. So unless you are aiming for a place in the Guinness World Records as the person winning the most arguments, then choose your battles. Remember, 'Don't sweat the small stuff!' The word of God in Proverbs 19:11 says, *A person's wisdom yields patience. It is to one's glory to overlook an offense*. Agree early in your marriage what you consider to be "big stuff." Some common ones are infidelity, abuse, and neglect. Set mutually accepted boundaries. Talk about these things. Never assume your partner will always know how his actions will affect you. Having agreed on what constitutes the big stuff, you may have to tolerate the other stuff.

You do not need to win every argument. In my early teens, I learned this quote: "Why win an argument and lose a friend?" Your spouse should be your closest friend. Protect that friendship. You will not see eye to eye with your partner on everything. It will not happen. Remember you are coming from different backgrounds, or even if similar backgrounds it is unlikely that you both would have been exposed to the same influences in the same degree and have responded in the same way!

Your partner will do things that annoy you and vice versa. But I have heard women who lose their husbands through some tragedy, express that they would gladly tolerate those annoyances in exchange for the return of their husbands. Don't wait until you have such an experience to start realizing that the minor annoyances such as leaving the toilet seat up, or squeezing the toothpaste from the middle will pale in comparison to the pain of losing your husband. You have this opportunity to not allow minor differences in preference or even annoying habits become an issue. Part of the happiness of life consists not in fighting battles, but in avoiding them. A masterly retreat is in itself a victory. (Norman Vincent Peale)

22. Watch The Criticism: Praise Ratio ♥

I have yet to find a man, however exalted his station, who did not do better work and put forth greater effort under a spirit of approval than under a spirit of criticism. Charles Schwab

The bible says in Proverbs 16:24, *Pleasant words are like honeycomb, sweet to the soul and health to the bones*. It has been said that we hear thirty-two criticisms for each praise that we receive. If we are not careful, we will focus on the negative things in our relationships and rarely speak about the positive. In fact, sometimes we even use scriptures to support our negative onslaught on each other.

We have to be deliberate about avoiding the trap of always criticising our spouse. Rather, we should practice Mathew 7:3 - taking the beam out of our eyes before seeing the mote in our spouse's. We must practice to restrain ourselves from criticising our spouse. It cannot be overemphasized. Criticism will suck the marrow from the bones of your relationship. It will make you unbearable. Your spouse will not enjoy sharing time and space with you. You will repel him.

You must recognise and accept that your spouse is human and will do some things poorly. It will happen, not once, not twice, not thrice. The fact is, you too do some things poorly. And you know how uncomfortable it is when you are being criticised. It is not a good feeling.

On the other hand, every opportunity you get to express admiration for an act, irrespective of how simple or unimportant the act may seem, you should communicate it to your spouse. For example, you could tell your spouse that you admire his skill at driving or that he preached a good sermon or he is a skilful lover!

While there may be many instances where you could criticise your husband, if you look hard enough, there will always be something to praise him for as well. Choose the latter and enhance the intimacy in your relationship. So the next time you are tempted to criticise your spouse, I encourage you to shut your mouth and bite your lip!

23. Me Time ♥

Be there for others, but never leave yourself behind.
Unknown

It is very important that you choose to spend some time with you - Just you. Note I did not say "find the time" as the usual response is that "I cannot find any time". You need time to stay in touch with the inner you – to ask yourself some questions and to answer them (No, I do not suggest that you do this in the earshot of anyone. They could call a psychiatrist!)

You should regularly ask yourself questions such as:

Am I growing? (Not physically of course). Am I living on purpose or merely existing? What season of life am I in? What should I expect in this season? Am I fulfilled? Is there anything I could do differently to improve my wellbeing? How is my relationship with my God? Am I spending reasonable time with Him? These are but a few examples of the questions you should ask yourself.

So while this soul searching may not be necessary on a daily basis, you should do something that you like everyday... even if it is as simple as reading a book or having a cup of tea without being disturbed or without thinking about what you will be doing when you have finished drinking the tea! You must practice to recharge your batteries. Almost everything will work again, if you unplug it for a few minutes... including you. (Anne Lamott)

Sometimes as women we believe that we are being very noble by taking care of he, she, and the old lady (everyone) and burning ourselves out. We believe that the world will fall apart if we are not in control. Well, my dear, many of our sisters with that philosophy are no longer with us today. And guess what? The world is still here.

So schedule some me time every day. Do something you like. You will be a happier person and thus a happier wife!

24. Half A Muffin ♥

Make it your habit not be critical about small things. Unknown

Half a muffin. Half a carrot muffin to be exact! That is what my husband brought for me one evening as I was working late. Now if after over twenty years of marriage your husband chose to drive to your office to give you half of a muffin, it means the chemistry is still strong. You might disagree with me. You could be saying to yourself - half a muffin! You may even hiss your teeth and ask, "What is this?" if you were in my position. But never make that mistake. That kind of response kills the spirit. It "kills vibes" and embarrasses the giver.

Never miss an opportunity to respond with gratitude to an act of kindness, irrespective of how small you may perceive that act to be. It does not matter that you believe more could be done. In my muffin case, it may be natural to think he should have stopped somewhere to get me more food! Well I chose to respond with gratitude and tenderness on what I perceived to be an act of kindness. 1 Thessalonians 5:18 exhorts us, *In everything give thanks*. This is by no means an easy instruction to follow. It is not in our human nature to give thanks for anything that displeases us. It takes discipline and self-control.

Before you engage your mouth or roll your eyes, think how your partner is likely to react to your actions. So, in my muffin case, had I made a fuss that I came all the way from my office (which is upstairs) to a parking lot for half a muffin, my husband would probably be upset that he wasted his time and gas to bring me something for which I was not grateful! This could then lead to tension when we got home.

We have to be careful that we do not allow little things (like a half muffin) to cause big rifts in our marriage. When we trace the origin of many problems in marriage, we often find that little things were allowed to escalate into big issues. It is just not worth it. The enemy must know that if he is going to cause a problem in your marriage, he will have to come big, real big!

25. Understanding, Sympathetic, Or Plain Tolerant ♥

Even the most fickle are faithful to a few bad habits.
Mason Cooley

I am convinced that each of us has a habit (may be more than one) which is so ingrained in us that irrespective of how hard we try, the habit remains. Even the Apostle Paul seemed to be able to relate. In Romans 7:19 he said, *For the good that I would I do not: but the evil which I would not, that I do.* The fact is, oftentimes having been convinced that a habit is not good, we change for a season, only to return to our old, undesirable habit.

If we are honest, we all can identify even one such habit in our own lives. Now, if that is true, let's say, that one habit is also annoying your spouse. How would you want him to deal with you on the issue, considering that you also wished that you didn't have the habit? Maybe you would wish that he'd be understanding, sympathetic or just plain tolerant? That seems reasonable.

Well, whichever way you wished for him to act, you should also act in the same way to his annoying habits. You have to choose to be understanding, sympathetic or just plain tolerant.

Seek God's grace to help you cope. 2 Corinthians 12:19 tells us that God's grace is sufficient. It truly is. We just need to open up our spirits and allow Him to work through us. We cannot do it in our own strength. We do need the Lord's help. Ask God for a healthy dose of understanding, compassion and tolerance. Our partners are imperfect beings. We therefore need to program our minds and attitudes to deal with our partner's imperfections that will inevitably surface.

It is important however that you do not suffer abuse in your relationship under the guise that you are being tolerant. Tolerance has limits! Abuse is off limits!

26. Prioritize Him ♥
Your schedule reveals your priorities. Unknown

I have heard many women passionately declaring, "Mi nah put no man before mi pickney." (I will not prioritize a man over my child). Invariable when this is said, it is followed by some tirade against the man. It is usually that these women have had negative experiences with men or they know someone who has.

So while I cannot deny the realities of these women, the word of God in 1 Corinthians 11:3 says: ...*the head of every man is Christ; and the head of the woman is the man*... 1 Timothy 3:4 also says, *A man should rule his household well*. The word of God clearly puts the man at the head of the household. So if the bible puts the man at the head, then clearly the children should not be above him. If we adhere to biblical principles, it follows that your husband should be prioritized over your children.

Now before smoke starts coming out of your ears, prioritizing your husband does not mean that you put his needs ahead of your children to their detriment. Certainly not! But it does mean setting a tone in your house where everyone, including the children, honours your husband as head of the family. Treating him with respect; not speaking disparagingly to or about your husband in the hearing of your children are basic examples. It doesn't matter if he is saved or unsaved. In fact, if he is unsaved you have more reason to honour him: It is by your chaste conduct that he could be won for Christ. (1Peter 3:1)

On the issue of unsaved husbands, many women who attend church make a grave mistake. They believe that they are really serving God when they leave their husbands to attend church every day of the week including twice on Sundays! Read my lips: it's not biblical! You are setting up your marriage for failure. You must make time for your husband. (Or someone else will!) Stay home with him and rub his head, cut his nails or squeeze pimples (even imaginary ones!).

Another issue which I would like to raise is that of fasting. Do you know that you should seek your husband's (saved or unsaved) permission to go on fasting? Yes, read 1 Corinthians 7:5 - It says: *Do not deprive one another except with consent for a time, that you may give yourselves to fasting and prayer*. When you seek your husband's consent before proceeding to fast, you are not only adhering to the word of God but you are demonstrating to your husband that you honour him.

And what if he does not act in a way worthy of honour, you may ask? Or, he does not prioritize you? My simple answer is that he will have to give an account of his actions and so will you! So what will your account look like? Do you unhesitatingly respond to requests made of you by those whom you consider respectable such as your pastor or a senior person, but you have to think twice before responding to a request from your spouse? Could your husband be silently wishing you would treat him the way you treat these persons? If we are honest, we are guilty of sometimes giving precedence to our jobs, children, friends, interests, even church activities over our spouse. *Letter 82 – How is my Wife-ing* suggests we obtain feedback from our spouse as to our performance as a wife. At that time you could ask if he feels that you prioritize him.

If you think that he does not prioritize you, you should let him know. If you cannot resolve the issue, then the marriage is in trouble and needs professional help.

27. It's Not Good For The Man To Be Alone 💔

Loneliness and the feeling of being unwanted is the most terrible poverty. Mother Theresa

In Genesis 2:18 the Lord God said: *It is not good that the man should be alone; I will make him an help meet for him.* I hear so many married persons complain about being lonely. One of the reasons persons get married is to satisfy the need for companionship. We must therefore be very careful how we fill our lives with activities that exclude our spouses. While it is certainly not wise to spend every single moment of every single day with your spouse (you do need breathing space), you should plan your days, having considered your spouse's need of your company. It is easy to fall in a routine without any consideration of the impact your schedule is having on your marriage.

According to Willard F Harley Jr. one of the basic needs of men is recreational companionship. This belief is certainly in line with Genesis 2:18. The Lord did not intend for the man to be alone. So it's important that your spouse knows that he is important enough for you to consider him in your schedule. It may mean that you have to schedule quality time with your spouse. This is especially important if quality time is your spouse's love language.

The bible says in Ephesians 4:27: *Do not give place to the devil.* I believe that when we fill our schedule and leave little time for our spouse, we run the risk of giving place to the devil. Your husband could start to feel neglected and the enemy could provide him with alternative company. That company could prove ruinous to your marriage. So be careful to do everything in your power to provide company to your husband as it's not good for the man to be alone.

28. Validate His Feelings ♥

The key to unlock your spouse's heart is validation. Unknown

Feelings need not be logical, practical or even reasonable. Emotions are too complex to try to reduce them to categories of reasonable and unreasonable. Feelings are often times inexplicable, but that does not make them any less valid. That's just the way it is. You cannot dictate how another person should feel. In fact, sometimes not even the persons themselves can explain why they feel the way they do.

You therefore have to learn to respond or adjust your actions to how your partner is feeling. It is pointless to argue that he should not feel the way he is feeling. One of the most important things to remember is that you must validate your partner's feelings. Some remarks to avoid are: "you shouldn't feel that way" - or worse - "I wouldn't feel that way." What you are actually doing is setting up yourself as the standard by which others should be judged. That kind of attitude erodes the fabric of the relationship.

You should try to create an atmosphere where your partner feels comfortable to share his feelings without fear of being judged - or worse- of being ridiculed. I have heard many women complain that their husbands "do not talk", meaning that they do not share their inner most feelings with them. While some men find it extremely difficult to express their inner most feelings, some just refrain from doing so. They simply cannot be bothered with the instructions from their spouse on how they should feel.

Instead of criticising or instructing your husband on how he should feel, try to understand his feelings and why he may be feeling that way. Sometimes a different perspective can evoke a different feeling. So there may be times when you can show him a different perspective and he may feel differently. But even in those circumstances, you must first validate his feelings. His feelings do not have to make sense to you. If we are honest, sometimes our feelings do not make sense to us!

So if your husband comes home and is complaining to you about a matter, and for the life of you, you cannot see why he should be upset, please resist the temptation to interrupt him and instruct him on how he should feel!

Try to empathize with your spouse's feelings and if you can't, then just shut up!

29. Make Him Look Good ♥
In honour, preferring one another. Romans 12:10

The bible says in Matthew 19:6 that *the two shall become one*. It therefore means that if your spouse looks good, you look good. Unfortunately, the converse is also true. But let's focus on the positive. You should never feel the need to compete with your spouse (unless of course it's in a game or purely for fun).

Always be prepared to support your spouse in whatever way you can in keeping with his needs. The support could range from simple things like reminding him of special dates for his family members or helping him with an important speech. Your opinion on whether what he is going to do is a big deal or not, is unimportant. Providing it is important to him, then help him succeed. Your partner should be better off for having married you.

Your attitude should not be one of "you-had-better-thank-God-for-me" because "you-succeed-only-because-of-me." Rather it should be one of gratitude to be sharing the life of another person and having the privilege to help. Furthermore, you should consider that in the game of life, you are both on the same team. One very good definition of the word team that I have come across is: T-together, E-each, A-achieves,

M-more! The key word there being together. When you unite, you both look better.

Having done all you can to make him into a success, you must now resist the need to inform "the world and his wife" that you are the one who helped him to succeed. Everyone already knows the very popular quote, "Behind every successful man is a woman." No need to shove him out of the way and shout, "I'm the reason for his success!"

30. He Did Not Marry His Mother 🖤

Three things drive a man outdoors: smoke, a leaking roof and a scolding wife. Unknown

Women are wired to not only nurture and care, but to instruct and direct. As mothers, we give direction and instruction to our children. That is our prerogative; our duty, even. But we must be careful, in fact, very careful, when it comes to our husbands!

They are not our children. They are not children (even if their actions belie the fact!) We should not constantly instruct our spouse. Some women make the mistake of always giving their spouse directions and instructions without even asking their opinions. When we constantly do that we run the risk that they will simply stop thinking. Stop caring. Why should they? We do all the thinking for them. We are the authority on all subjects! We are always instructing them. It is a dangerous practice and it will backfire.

Each spouse has strengths and weaknesses. And you may have strengths in areas where he is weak. That does not give you the right to "boss" him or order him around. Never forget that he is an adult. He must be treated as one at all times. Ephesians 5:33 tells us to reverence our husbands. In fact, Sarah called her husband, lord! I recall visiting a couple to counsel with them. During the session, the wife was scolding her husband. After the session I called her and asked how many sons she had. I already knew they had only one child, but I wanted to bring home my point. When she answered one, I said I didn't believe, because she treated her husband like her son. As she reflected on my comment she broke down in tears.

It will be tempting to scold, instruct and talk down to your husband especially when he does anything you deem childish. But there is never a justifiable reason to treat your spouse like your child. He did not marry his mother!

31. When You Marry Down ♥
Do to others, what you would have them do to you. Matthew 7:12

It is very rare, that a woman marries a man only to help him, and nothing else (though some women swear that is what happened - well business marriages excluded). Nevertheless, having married him, I believe she will derive some benefit, however little she may perceive it to be.

With this view in mind, I do not think that a woman should have a superiority complex simply because she may be more educated, financially sound or older than her spouse. Once you get married, it is important to see your spouse as not only your equal, but the head of your household and treat him accordingly. When you "look down" on your spouse, it is the beginning of the end for your marriage.

Keep reminding yourself why you agreed to marry him. Did you simply need the use of his penis because you wanted a family? Well it is grossly unfair if he kept his end of the bargain and you want to renege. Oh, I know life is unfair, but why do you want to be the one to go back on your vows? Ecclesiastes 5:5 says, "It is better not to vow than to make one and not fulfil it.

Learn to see yourself as his helpmeet, then you will seek to elevate him. I see you rolling your eyes, shaking your head and thinking that you have tried several times to elevate him and he is a hopeless case! He will not change overnight. It takes time. And you need to remember you are not the one who will change him. He will have to make the decision for himself.

If you are truly honest, most, if not all of the flaws which now annoy the H-E-2-STICKS out of you were evident before you said "I do."

You therefore need to seek God's face and His grace. You also need to pray for coping skills.

It makes no sense to nag him about his flaws. Believe me, it will only drive a wedge between you. Try to think of his positive attributes. (Said many times before). Someone once said that we can't live a positive life with a negative mind. Philippians 4:8 tells us that we are to think on the things that are true, right, pure, lovely admirable excellent or praiseworthy. I have no doubt that your spouse has positive attributes. He has at least one; his good judgement led him to marrying you. Right?

32. Respect Due ♥

Respect is what we owe; love is what we give.
Phillip James Bailey

Our respect for our spouse must guide our words and actions. Whether we agree or disagree with our spouse, under no circumstances should he be disrespected. Many women make the grave mistake of belittling their spouses. Some even go as far as referring to them as idiots. Of course it begs the question - does it mean he is an idiot for marrying you? And what about you – what does it say for you as his wife to have agreed to marry an idiot? Our partner will from time to time display poor judgement (you may be tempted to say 'not from time to time' it's all the time!). Well the next question would be, was he like this before marriage? If he was like this before marriage, then why complain? Why make it an issue if you were aware of his proclivity for poor judgement?

And what if it is since you married? Well, maybe you have to take a long hard look at your influence on him. Could it be that you are contributing to his poor decisions? The issue here is that whether you believe he makes more than his fair share of poor decisions or not, you should not consider the option to disrespect him. It is as simple as that. Respect is due all the time.

Believe me, if your partner does make many poor decisions, he will have enough persons outside your marriage who will disrespect him. You do not need to add to the number. 1Peter 2:17 says we should show proper respect to everyone" That 'everyone' certainly includes your husband!

33. Speak To The King, Not The Fool ♥

Every wife is a king-maker. Mathew Jacobson

Someone once said that there is a king and a fool in every man. If you speak to the king, the king will respond, but if you speak to the fool, the fool will respond. I therefore encourage you to always speak to the king in your husband. (Even if he is acting like a fool!)

How different our actions would be if we reverenced our husband enough to think of him as a king. I believe we would choose our words wisely in addressing him; we would watch our tone of voice, we would watch our body language; we would watch how we dress for him (Remember Esther?) We would watch how we treat him in general.

We should think carefully about what emotions our words and actions could evoke from our spouse. How will he feel about what you did or said? Maya Angelou said:

> *People will forget what you said*
>
> *People will forget what you did*
>
> *But people will never forget how*
>
> *You made them feel*

I therefore encourage you to think of your husband as a king and treat him accordingly. Remember the way you treat him should not be influenced by his behaviour (especially if it is negative) but by your decision. I know this is a hard pill to swallow but you must train yourself to do the things that are unnatural. As Christians, we are not called to be natural, but to walk in the Spirit, to do the things that please the Lord and bring glory and honour to Him. Sometimes we have to struggle with our flesh to do the things we know are right. Romans 8:8 tells us that they that are in the flesh cannot please God.

So think of yourself as the queen you are and if you are a queen then your husband is the king. And if he is a king, then treat him accordingly!

34. He Is Not Jesus

*My soul wait thou only upon God,
from him cometh my expectation. Psalms 62:5*

The song writer says "All that I need is in Jesus." Note he said "Jesus." Not in your partner. Your partner cannot and will not be able to supply all your needs at all times. Maybe he will be able to meet all your physical needs, but certainly not your emotional and spiritual needs. He is not Jesus. There are some things that only a deep relationship with the Lord can satisfy. In bible days, only the priest could enter the holiest of holies to offer sacrifices for sins. He had to go alone. This same principle still applies. Some emotional needs can only be met when you enter the holiest of holies to commune with God. It is therefore imperative that you recognise and accept the limitation of your human partner.

Don't be too frustrated if he doesn't understand you as well as you would like him to. The truth of the matter is that we don't know ourselves as well as we think we do. Remember the Lord and Peter? The Lord told Peter that he would deny Him three times before the cock crowed. Of course Peter "took Jesus off the cross" declaring that he would never do that. However, Peter did deny Jesus three times before the cock crowed. (Matthew 26:75)

It is unreasonable and downright puerile to expect your partner to always say the right things in the right way at the precise time you want it said or to always do the right things in the right way at the precise time you want it done. It is just not going to happen. You must look to God to satisfy your needs. He is your source. Your husband is a channel. God can use any channel to supply your needs. Do not expect your partner to supply all your needs. He is not Jesus!

35. He's No Mind Reader ♥
You lose more than you can imagine by not saying anything at all.
Unknown

While your spouse may at times accurately guess what you are thinking, it will not and cannot happen all the time. It is therefore imperative that you express your feelings and thoughts, what you like and dislike; what you expect and do not expect. You also need to communicate when you have changed your mind.

As women, we change our minds in a split second and we expect our spouses to know when we have changed our minds without telling them. This is recipe for conflict as your spouse may well believe that what he is doing or saying is pleasing you. If you change your mind about a previous decision, or maybe you no longer enjoy something that you do together or a gift he usually gives to you, do find a gentle way to say you no longer enjoy the activity or the gift. Note I said "a gentle way." Some of us are very good at making our men feel like idiots.

We think to ourselves that if he loved me enough he should know what I like or what I am thinking even though we are changing our minds more rapidly than the blink of an eye.

So tell your spouse how you are feeling. Unexpressed emotions will never die. They are buried alive and will come forth in uglier ways. (Sigmund Freud).

I know some men may not express themselves to their spouse, but that is no reason for you not to express yourself. At least he will not have the excuse of saying he did not know what you were thinking. So tell him what you want him to know as he is not a mind reader. You may have to tell him over and over. But that's another issue!

36. Choose To Trust ♥

Judge not, lest ye be judged. Matthew 7:1

There are times when you may be uncomfortable with some actions of your partner. You may be uneasy about something he is doing or something you suspect he is doing. My recommendation is that you first seek God's face about the matter. Spend time before God praying about your suspicion. Never voice your suspicion as if it were a proven fact.

Remember when the angel appeared before Mary and told her that she was going to conceive? The bible said Mary *pondered these things in her heart* (Luke 2:19) She must have turned it over in her mind a million times.

The difficulty with suspicion is that it can eat you alive. It will affect everything your partner does or says. If you do not have concrete proof to support your suspicion, it is better to choose to believe that your partner is innocent of your suspicion and ask God to deal with him if he is in fact guilty.

However, you should ask him about any actions with which you are uncomfortable. For example, if he suddenly starts to go out without you and comes home late, the natural thing to do would be to accuse him of having an affair. Resist the urge to accuse him of having an affair, but certainly let him know how you feel about him coming home late. So focus on something that you both know is true, rather than a suspicion that may not be true.

If you accuse your partner and he is innocent, that can destroy your marriage. Your partner will know that you do not trust him and a relationship cannot survive without trust. Someone once said, "A relationship without trust is like a car without gas, you can stay in it all you want, but it won't go anywhere." So my dear, sometimes you simply have to choose to trust.

37. This Business Of Sex ♥

Research consistently shows that between 80 and 90 percent of men view sex as the most important aspect of their marriage. Julie Slattery

From the outset of your marriage, you need to develop a certain attitude to sex.

Here is something worth considering: if your husband needs food, he can take his pick from numerous restaurants. If he needs his clothes laundered, he can use the laundromat or hire someone. If he needs the house cleaned, helpers abound. When he wants sex, should he have to wait until you are in the mood? Or should he also find an alternative?

Now before your blood boil, I do believe that your husband should control himself as there will be times when you are certainly not up to engaging in sex. But it cannot be that he should only have sex when you are in the mood. Something is wrong with that picture. Neither should he have to enjoy only wilderness sex; that is only after forty days and forty nights!

One of the best definitions of sexual intercourse I came across is the giving and or receiving of pleasure. That means sometimes you will only give pleasure. Sometimes you will only be the one getting pleasure. (I think this is very rare though).

At other times, you both will enjoy the sex act. The same way you plan your food menu for your family to make sure they are fed, it's the same way you must plan to give your husband sex as he has no other right way of getting it! I remember asking a sister if she asked her husband if he wanted sex. She asked me if I was crazy. In fact, the way she looked at me told me she was thinking that she always suspected that something was wrong with me. Now her doubts were settled!

One preacher says that a man does not want sex, he needs sex to function. He said sex to a man is what fuel is to a car. While the analogy may seem a little extreme, it would be helpful to bear it in mind so it can guide your attitude to sex.

You are not ready for marriage if you think sex is a trivial thing or something that couples may do once in a while. That may be your perception, but I am yet to meet a man who thinks sex is a trivial matter. Even for the bible thumping preacher sex is a serious matter.

Sex is such a serious matter that the bible in 1 Corinthians 7:5 instructs couples not to deprive each other, except it's by mutual consent for a time. Note it says by mutual consent. So develop an attitude which says you are conscious of the fact you are the only one with whom your husband can rightfully engage in sex. Develop the attitude which says your husband's appetite for sex is far greater than yours. That's just the way it is!

38. No Right To Say "No" ♥

*Let her be as the loving hind and pleasant roe;
let her breasts satisfy thee at all times; and be thou ravished always
with her love. Proverbs 5:19*

I have been asked many times if a wife has a right to say "No" when her husband asks her for sex. My simple answer is usually *No*.

My simple answer is based on 1 Corinthians 7:4, which says,

The woman does not have power over her own body but the husband. Now before the feminist blood in you boil, the verse continues on to say, *The husband does not have power over his own body, but the wife.*

I am not sure that will cool you down, but please try. I believe that the word of God is trying to get husbands and wives to a place where they commit to satisfy each other's needs. It is important to recognize that you have the exclusive right to satisfy the sexual needs of your partner. Now does it mean that every single time that your husband wants sex you must accommodate him? No, that's not what I'm saying. But your attitude must communicate to him that you recognise his right to your body even if for some reason you are not able to satisfy his needs at that time. It cannot be that you "lock shop" and shun him simply because you are not in the mood or you do not think he deserves it.

There will be times that you simply cannot participate in sex. However you must cultivate a relationship that your partner can easily recognise that you genuinely cannot have sex at that time. You should also explicitly share your reason and do not assume that he should know. If you are sick and the world knows it and he ask for sex, then you are probably married to a very selfish person. That's another issue. Even then, remind him that you would if you could and promise him a rain cheque. It serves no useful purpose to curse him and tell him how selfish he is (though that is the most natural thing to do!)

You may not be sick, but just not in the mood. Maybe you lost your job, or some possession or you are feeling stressed or disappointed. If your partner is aware of how you are feeling and still wants sex, then you may have to send a quick prayer to your Father upstairs and ask Him for grace and more grace. You need to ask Him to remind you that men can compartmentalize their lives. Yes, they may be sorry that you lost your job or some possession or that you may be disappointed about some matter, but as far as they are concerned, they are two different issues. While your mind may be totally consumed with how you will manage in the future, they are operating in the moment: You are available and able to have sex!

It will take all the self-control and then some, not to shun him! But God's grace is sufficient. Call on Him. It's no wonder that 1Thessalonians 5:17 tells us to *pray without ceasing*. It's in circumstances like these we recognize the wisdom of those words!

So the main point of this letter is: attitude is everything. You must communicate to your partner that you embrace 1 Corinthians 7:4, that is, you know that he has power over your body and in those times when you cannot meet his sexual needs, you will graciously let him know.

Now, I have to say that 1 Corinthians 7:4 is not saying that your husband has the right to abuse you or do whatever he will with your body. In my mind, if he crosses the line to abuse, then he loses his right to your body. The word of God says in Ephesians 5:28 that *men ought to love their wives as their own bodies.* There is absolutely no place in marriage for abuse - real or imagined.

39. Sex Is Your Right Too ♥

.....if ye find my beloved, tell him, that I am sick of love.
Solomon 5:8

Too many wives are of the notion that sex is a man's thing. They are even embarrassed to admit that they too have sex urges. Well let me make it clear, while the men may be the head of the sex urge department, you were also wired to desire sex and you should acknowledge and embrace those urges. I have no doubt that you will know when your husband is in the mood for sex. But what happens when you are in the mood? You should sit quietly by and pray that your husband will somehow know and initiate the act? Oh no! Not so! Sex is your right too.

While I do not suggest that you hit him over the head, drag him in the bedroom and demand sex (although some husbands would welcome such an action), I encourage you to communicate your urge to your husband. In fact, there are very few husbands who would not be flattered if their wives initiated sex for a change. When you make the move, you are saying to your man I want you baby. That's music to his ears!

You can communicate covertly or cut to the chase and say exactly what you want. A friend once told me that whenever she suggests to her husband that they take a shower together, he knows exactly what's on her mind. But your husband may not recognise the subtle invitation and may suggest that you take your shower first and then he will take his later! Or you may say you are thirsty and he offers you a drink. In that case you may just have to say it as plain as day. You could say something like "Horny... I mean honey, I really do need some love making right now!" Of course you may have created your own nickname for love making. Most couples do.

The bottom line is to create your unique way to communicate to your husband your need for sex and dispel the notion that you must sit back and wait until he is in the mood. Sex is your right too!

40. Stay In The Moment ♥

*If you have your full attention in the moment,
you will see only love. Unknown*

I received an email with two images. The first one had hundreds of balls moving around in several directions. The second image had only two balls going in one direction. The caption of the first picture read, "The mind of a woman" while the caption of the second picture read -- I'm sure you guessed it - "The mind of a man."

I am sure the images were meant to be primarily humorous, but they also conveyed a valid truth. Some of us ladies are always thinking about several things. Even during sex our minds cannot be still! I heard a story about a wife suggesting to her husband during sexual intercourse that they could change the colour of the ceiling! What a turn off!

My dear, while I am not suggesting you moan and groan in false ecstasy, you should focus your mind on what is happening so you can participate meaningfully. There will be times when you are not able to, or just not in the mood to participate, but these times should be rare. Pull back your mind each time it strays. Inwardly pray and ask God to help you stay in the moment.

NB. Please don't ever make the mistake of praying out loud!

If you practice to stay in the moment, you may find that you enjoy sex more. In addition, I have heard that sex is said to offer many health benefits such as pain relief, stress relief, lowering of blood pressure and improved sleep. You should not rob yourself of these health benefits, so stay in the moment and enjoy the benefits!

41. Raising The Dead ♥

There is nothing stronger in the world than gentleness. Unknown

While most men will not admit it, there will be times when their penis (let's call it Lazarus) will not function. It will not "stand up."

It will be dead...

Dead!

The condition is called erectile dysfunction (ED). Stress, fatigue, medical conditions, medications and anxiety are some underlying causes. Some may be able to function for only a short time. Whatever the situation is, a malfunctioning penis strikes at the heart of your husband's manhood. It is a very sensitive issue.

You must therefore exercise an abundance of understanding, patience and skill. I say skill because if Lazarus is dead as a result of anxiety, you can use your charm to put your husband at ease. Reassure both him and Lazarus that they need to relax. Yes, you should also talk to Lazarus. Tell him you know he wants to please you and you are willing to wait until he is ready (even though inside you may be dying for action). Stroke him gently until he responds.

You must develop a relationship with Lazarus. 1 Corinthians 7:4 tells us, *Likewise also the husband hath not power of his own body, but the wife*. In other words, the man's body belongs to the woman. That means every part! If malfunctioning Lazarus is not due to some serious underlying illness, then a little tenderness, patience and understanding will usually raise the dead.

If the problem is prolonged then you must encourage your husband to go to the doctor and get help. Remember it is a very sensitive issue for him and so you must be very patient and gentle. You should also solicit the help of the Lord. I believe in praying about everything! James 5:16 tells us that the prayer of a righteous person is powerful and effective. So seek God's help. After all, the Lord did raise Lazarus from the dead!

42. Sex: The Effective Anaesthetic 🖤

There is a huge amount of freedom that comes to you when you take nothing personally. Don Miguel Ruiz

I remember when I was to do a surgery, I was wheeled into the theatre and briefed on what would take place in the theatre. The anaesthetist told me she was going to put something over my nose and I should close my eyes and count slowly backwards from 100. I remember I started to count but I don't think I got very far. Soon I was out cold.

Well my dear, I am convinced that sex has the same power over a man as anaesthetic does. It simply knocks him out cold almost instantaneously after! Many wives complain that they feel used because their husbands simply go off to sleep after the act. However when they learn that it is a very common occurrence they feel a little better. So when this happens, do not take it personally, it is a man's thing. If you do not believe me, do your own survey. I couldn't believe that my husband could start to sleep (even snore) in less than a minute (and I am not exaggerating) after sex.

So if you expect company to lay awake with you to bask in the afterglow of great sex, let me warn, it is hardly likely to happen. Don't hold your breath! Enjoy your afterglow in solitude and use the time to thank God you have a man - your own man and not borrowed goods. Use the time to give thanks for all the positives in your life. Hopefully, you too will drift off into a fitful sleep and experience sweet dreams!

    I do believe that you should still share your desire for post-sex cuddling and conversation. But the point I am making is, if it doesn't happen, don't feel bad, it's really not about you. Just think of it as the anaesthetic power of sex!

43. To Spoon Or Not To Spoon ♥

Again, if two lie together, they keep warm, but how can one keep warm alone? Ecclesiastes 4:11

I've had men complain to me that their wives were not loving. They get no comfort from them. These men love to hug; to kiss; to snuggle. When they sleep they love to spoon. It's their comfort. But no, their wives want space! Well my dear Mrs. Right, if you do not like to spoon and your spouse does, shouldn't you ask yourself, "Can I accommodate him? At least some times..."

Marriage is about meeting each other's needs. Spooning may be one way your spouse feels close to you. In fact I doubt that he would want to spoon if he was upset with you! You could spoon for half the night and sleep apart for the other half. Negotiate. But never "run" him, or push him away while telling him he "loves to hug too much" Or worse yet, tell him: "you do not like him so close to you."

That would not be good. He could interpret it as rejection. And that you do not want. I know some of us were raised in families that were not affectionate, but you can choose to meet the needs of your partner. Hugging and spooning may just be some of his needs. I cannot repeat too often, that if you live your life purely on your feelings, you are robbing yourself and you will miss out on a far more fulfilling life. You have to choose to make decisions that benefit your marriage whether you feel to or not!

    You cannot only do the things that you like to do. You have to be mature enough to do somethings that you do not even like to do. So if your husband likes to spoon or knife or fork... would it kill you to accommodate him? (Well maybe you can forego the knife and fork since I'm not even sure how to do those).

44. Be Nice To Be Near ♥

For a man looketh on the outward appearance.
1 Samuel 16:7

Men are visual beings, so make sure you are deliberate about looking your best. It does not matter that you are in the house doing chores. Now do not get me wrong, I am not saying that you should dress in stockings and evening dress to do chores. What I am saying is, make some effort to look attractive. Ditch the old housedress. Ditch the old T-shirts with holes of all shapes and sizes. Ditch the old stocking covering your hair. Still act as you did when you were dating.

When you were dating, you would make extra effort to look attractive. You should make twice that effort to stay attractive. And it is not just about your husband, when you look good, you feel good.

Make sure that you are attractive when going to bed. If you live in a tropical country, like Jamaica, there is no need to cover up and bundle up. The long old nighties and old T-shirts and big shorts have no place in the bedroom. I care not how comfortable you are in them. Wear sexy underwear to bed. Men like to feel flesh. And not rough flesh. So use moisturizer and lotion to keep skin soft. If you can't afford those, use Vaseline!

Men are also attracted to smell. Smell nice. If you cannot afford perfumes, you can use body sprays. If you are allergic to perfumes or body sprays, at least smell clean. Be deliberate about smelling clean.

When your husband is in the mood to snuggle up to you and cuddle, resist the temptation to raise all the problems in the home, at the office, all the things he has not done that you asked him to. Just enjoy the moment. Allow him to simply enjoy being near you. Just be nice to be near!

45. Flirt It Baby! ♥

Some women flirt with what they say, and some with what they do.
Anna Held

Someone once said: "I'm not flirting, I'm being extra nice to someone who is extra attractive." One of the definitions of flirting is trying to attract the attention and admiration of someone for mere self-gratification. So, I say to you my sister, never stop flirting with your husband. I can imagine the expression on your holier-than-thou face! Well trust me, even if you think he makes King Kong look handsome or you have to use a magnifying glass to see his muscles, there are women (both saved and unsaved) who will flirt with him. And you know what? He may like it!

I believe flirting communicates to your husband, that 'hey, I still find you attractive and I am going to make myself attractive to keep your attention.' So make sure you are very deliberate about keeping yourself attractive. And it's not just physical attraction, but in the things you do and say. Be deliberate in being nice to him!

Listen to the things that he says he likes in other women. Listen to understand him more and not to accuse him of being unfaithful. Believe me, you do not possess all the qualities that your partner would love in a wife. Humbling, isn't it? And please do not ask him if you do. If you ask him, a smart man will always answer in the affirmative. Less stress! Fewer arguments! Moreover, for heaven's sake, when he says you do, please do not tell him he is lying - even though he is.

So be seductive. If he likes legs, then make sure he sees a lot of yours at home. If he likes breasts, then keep them attractive, even at home. I know some experts say we should take off our bra while we are at home, but that may not be so attractive especially if gravity is taking a toll on our breasts and they are now keeping company with our navel!

Solomon says in Solomon 4:9: *Thou hast ravished my heart, my sister, my spouse; thou hast ravished my heart with one of thine eyes, with one chain of thy neck...* Well whether you use; your eyes, neck, breasts, legs or any other body part for that matter, ravish his heart!

46. That Boyish Grin ♥
A happy heart makes the face cheerful. Proverbs 15:13

Every man, irrespective of his disposition, has a boyish grin. The challenge is to find out what evokes it and trigger it as often as possible.

I believe that every man, if taken to the place of true happiness will lose all inhibitions and behave a little crazy. In fact, some may even behave more than a little crazy. Whether he will do a crazy dance or song or something we may consider wild, it should be a wife's continuous desire to bring her husband to that position as often as possible. I believe it is a great feat when it is achieved. It is a great feeling when you know that you make your partner happy.

It is so sad to see so many unhappy couples. Most, if not everyone gets married believing that they will be happy. While the challenges of life are great, with a little determination and creativity you can make your partner grin.

Study your husband to know what makes him truly happy. In most cases, the answer will surround sex, either the offer of sex or performing some sex act. One preacher said that men think about sex every few seconds. While I have no evidence to support or refute that claim, very few men do not get excited about sex. They are wired that way. Except of course they believe you are using it to manipulate them.

So make a choice to do and say the things that will elicit that boyish grin. It is said that a happy wife makes for a happy life. Well, I believe that a happy husband makes for a happy life too. (Even though it doesn't rhyme!).

47. Think Like The Other Woman

Come to Me, all who are weary and heavy-laden, and I will give you rest. Mathew 11:28

I know you may shudder to even think that there could be another woman. Well my dear, while your Holy Ghost filled, water baptised, speaking-in-tongues husband may not engage in physical adulterous act, if you are not careful, and even when you are, he will at times wish he was in the company of another woman. Ooops! That may be a little damaging to your ego, but get over it. Your husband will likely prefer to be in the company of someone he can be himself with; someone who will not constantly nag him or remind him of all his shortcomings.

Proverbs 21:9 and Proverbs 25:24 admonish, *It is better to dwell in the corner of the house top than with a brawling woman in a wide house.* And Proverbs 21:19 says *It is better to dwell in the wilderness, than with a contentious and angry woman.* So while you may have very good reasons to be angry, be careful how you dish it out. You may just drive your husband out in the wilderness.

That wilderness may be the company of another woman. The other woman knows that her time with "the borrowed goods" is limited so she makes sure his experience is memorable. She makes sure his time with her is pleasant and who wouldn't prefer pleasant company to a nagging one! Think about it.

Do not take your husband for granted. Be deliberate in making him enjoy you. That means sometimes just forget about his short comings, forget about his annoying habits and just think about the ones that you truly like and enjoy. Remember Philippians 4:8 tells us: *Finally, brethren, whatsoever things are true, whatsoever things are honest, whatsoever things are just, whatsoever things are pure, whatsoever things are lovely, whatsoever things are of good report; if there be any virtue, and if there any praise, think on these things.*

48. Never Take Him For Granted ♥

Familiarity breeds contempt. Publilius Syrus

Have you ever noticed how we treat strangers? Especially the ones we deem somewhat important? With reverential respect! In fact, some are even held in awe! We hold these perfect strangers, who we know absolutely nothing about, in high regard. Yet the persons with whom we cohabit, we tend to treat with scant or no regard.

I am encouraging you to always treat your partner with deep respect, the same way you would treat a stranger that you deem important.

Always be polite, carefully choosing your words to say to your partner. Winston Churchill said, "We are masters of the words unsaid, but slaves to the ones we let slip out." You need to train yourself to think before you speak and act. Train yourself to consider how your words and action will affect your partner. Train yourself to think of the consequences of your words and actions. If it helps to keep your relationship in a respectful realm, then try at all times to think of your partner as a highly-respected stranger; and never get used to him. Never forget to display the simple courtesies: good morning, please, thank you. How are you?

    1 Peter 3:8 encourages us to *be ye all of one mind, having compassion one of another, love as brethren, be pitiful, be courteous,*

    Let it never be said that you treat a stranger with deeper respect than your husband. Remember Ephesians 5:33 says the wife should reverence her husband. And no, not only if you think he deserves it! It's an instruction to us as wives without qualification. Ask God for His grace to enable you to obey His word. When you think of it, it's really not about you and your husband... it's about your obedience to God's word. What could be more gratifying than knowing that you are pleasing the Lord by obeying His word?

49. His Cup Will Run Over ♥
Even the nicest people have their limits. Unknown

It is said that a man will not participate in a game if he knows for sure he will lose. Likewise, a man who believes that he can do nothing right by his wife will withdraw. He will simply not participate in the "game" of marriage. He may still perform certain duties, but there is no emotional connection with his spouse. He may even abandon the marriage when "his cup is full."

Never make the mistake of always treating your husband disrespectfully, belittling him or robbing him of his self esteem and believe that he will always stay with you. The bible says in Ephesians 4:15, *that we should speak the truth in love.*

You may not disrespect or belittle him but you nag and nag and nag! The things you are telling him (or nagging about) may be true (at least from your point of view), but no one wants to be nagged even if they are being told the truth.

Many wives who lose their husbands, say if given the chance, they would do and say things differently.

Proverbs 16:32 tells us that, *A person with self-control is better than one that conquers a city.* You have to practice to exercise self-control. You have to practice to resist the temptation to be always engaged in confrontation. (Unless of course you are really trying to frustrate your husband, so that he will abandon the marriage!)

It is a delicate balancing act, which you have to do. You have to choose your battles very carefully. If you choose to take on every battle, you may win then all, but lose your husband! His cup will run over.

50. The Time Should Fit The Crime ♥

That which is altogether just shall thou follow.
Deuteronomy 16:20

As issues arise in your marriage there will be times when you have to ask yourself, "Is this a big issue?" Or merely a difference in opinion or taste?

Many wives like to 'punish' their husbands by withholding sex for the slightest reason. He did not take out the garbage- no sex. He did not pay a bill – doghouse. Some other minor infraction caused by a lapse in memory – shop locked! But are these issues "big" enough matters for which to withhold sex? Surely, you will not be in the mood to be all lovey-dovey when you are upset. But you must resist from "punishing" your husband for every little misdeed!

It will take some training - training of your mind that is. Training yourself to be reasonable, even when you do not feel like being reasonable. Sex is fundamental to a marriage and many husbands are in a sexless marriage because they seem to have a penchant for upsetting their wives. So they upset their wives (and for some, it takes nothing to get their wives upset!) and they get no sex. Full stop. This can be very frustrating, especially for Christian husbands who are trying to remain faithful to God.

The fact is, sometimes they do not even try to please their wives because they believe that they will never succeed. So he doesn't try to please her, she withholds sex. She withholds sex, he doesn't try to please her. And the cycle continues. Before you know it, the marriage is reduced to acrimonious interactions only, or at best cold and civil communication.

Proverbs 10:6 says, *Blessings are upon the head of the just...* We should practice to be just, lest we thwart our own blessings! It shouldn't be that a wife withholds sex for the slightest annoyance when sex was fundamental to the decision to get married in the first place.

Let's not fool ourselves, one of the main reasons, if not the main one, that a Christian man marries is for sex; even if he will not admit it. And if your husband is not a Christian, then he may easily yield to the temptation to break his wedding vows and seek sex outside the marriage. So I encourage you to think twice before you 'punish' your husband by withholding sex.

51. Opposites Attract, But May Later Repel ♥

The happiest couples never have the same character; they just have the best understanding of their differences. Unknown

It is not unusual for us to be attracted to someone different from us. In fact, many find it intriguing. But those same qualities which were once admired can become irritating and a source of friction in many relationships. It takes mature - and I mean very mature persons - to be honest and admit that it's not their partner who has changed.

So for example, when you were courting, your then suitor sent you flowers very often; for no significant reason. You were the envy of many women who only dreamt of having a man send them flowers. So that made you feel real good. But fast forward; you are now married with bills to pay, maybe children to care for and very important expenses to meet. Your romantic husband still sends you flowers every week, but has no money to pay the utility bills!

I can see the colour of your skin changing even as you say to yourself no one would do that because that would not make sense. But I ask, make sense to whom? To your romantic husband, it makes perfect sense. As far as he is concerned, he is thinking of pleasing his lovely wife. He is thinking she will think of me as being oh so romantic and will be ready to "pay" me for these flowers in a rousing night of love-making. But you are outraged!

Of course you should tell him how you feel about the issue, but he may not see things your way. You would then need to speak to yourself. That is if you will listen to you! Remind yourself that people think differently. Remind yourself of all the good qualities that your partner has. And don't say it will hurt your brain trying to find one good quality...

Engage the Holy Spirit to assist you to control your rage or disappointment. Remember the wrath of man worketh not the righteousness of God (James 1:20).

So continue to wrestle until you get your breakthrough. You will either change your perspective or be given sufficient grace to accept the situation. Believe me, God's grace is sufficient if you open your heart to it.

You have to reach the place where you accept that your partner may have certain qualities that will not change. So what do you do? "Change your thinking and it will change your life." (Unknown)

52. He Will Disappoint, Upset, Fail You ♥

He is not perfect. You aren't either. Bob Marley

Your wedding vows may have included the phrase, "till death do us part." It therefore means that the intention (at least on the wedding day) is that you will be partners sharing the journey of life together.

That journey could be many, many years of togetherness. The quality of that life together will be influenced by your expectations of your partner. How realistic are those expectations? The reality is that if you expect that your spouse will never disappoint, upset or fail you then you are setting yourself up for disappointment and grief. He will disappoint you. He will upset you. He will fail you...

Let that sink in.

You therefore need to develop a strategy beforehand about how you will act or react when there are such occurrences. The ideal thing is that you are in such control that you will not act in a way, which will cause you to be ashamed or feel guilty afterwards. You have to exercise self-control; great self-control.

Proverbs 16:32 tells us, *He that is slow to anger is better than the mighty; and he that ruleth his spirit than he that taketh a city.*

Know beforehand how you will "rule your spirit" when you get upset. It is not if you will get upset, it's when. You may decide to walk away and cool down so you can afterwards clearly articulate your feelings or you may want to speak to yourself until you "right" your spirit.

Whatever you choose to do, it is important that you are in control. When you are in control you are less likely to do or say something that you will later regret.

Never forget that Matthew 26:41 says that the flesh is weak. It's not only your flesh that is weak. So is your partner's. While your spouse should be held accountable for his actions, you need to accept that your spouse will disappoint, upset or fail you simply because he's human! You therefore need to temper your expectations of your spouse. He is not perfect, and neither are you.

53. Watch The Jesting ♥

"Let it not once be named among you as becometh saints; neither filthiness, nor foolish talking nor jesting. Ephesians 5: 3-4

I believe that one of the effective glues in a great marriage is humour. If you can get your partner to smile or better yet, to double over with laughter, you are definitely strengthening your marriage. Someone once said that it is difficult not to love those who always make you laugh. So laughter is very important in your marriage.

You must however be careful with your humour. You should never make fun of your spouse in a way that will cause him pain or embarrassment. You must be sensitive. In fact, your objective should be to make your spouse laugh and not to laugh at him.

OK sometimes you can laugh at him.

However, laughing at some insecurities that he has is not a good idea. So for example, if he is short or has a big nose, it is inadvisable to laugh at him and tease him about these things. The fact is, he will get a lot of teasing from others, you need not join the throng.

I have seen women who embarrass their spouse by pointing out some issue such as his smelly toes or bad breath. If he has a problem with smelly toes or bad breath, then it is your duty to lovingly point it out to him privately and to encourage him to get help to correct the problem.

There will be enough unkind persons in the world to make your husband feel bad. You should not be one of them. Ephesians 4:32 instructs us to be kind, tender hearted and loving. Your husband should be able to count on you to be kind to him.

54. The Litmus Test ♥

Every way of a man is right in his own eyes.
Proverbs 21:2

My children will tell you that they have never heard my husband and me quarrelling. And before the cynic in you stand up with arms akimbo, eyes rolling, please note that I did not say we do not disagree on anything; or that I do not drive him up a wall sometimes (and vice versa). What I am saying is that by the grace of God and constant practice, we have managed to exercise control when we get upset. In most cases, if not all, we can feel the anger rising within us when we get upset. The challenge is how to deal with the anger responsibly. It takes practice, self-control, speaking to ourselves and an understanding of human nature.

One test I usually apply to any upsetting situation is to ask myself if it is a normal (though upsetting) human behaviour. I also ask myself if it could be proven that I too am guilty of the very same annoying thing (even if not in action, but in attitude).

For example, I often tell my husband that he should not fall asleep on the sofa leaving the television and lights on. He agrees. It may not happen for a day or two, then - you guessed it - he is back to his default position; television watching him with lights on. So my reaction is this: I ask myself, "Is it normal for someone to know when they are about to fall asleep and as such get up and do what they should?" I think yes and no. I think most persons know when they are about to fall asleep but they will not necessarily get up. After all, it has happened to me before - rarely of course - but it has happened. So, I don't let it be an issue. Yes, I may have to pay a little more for electricity bill, but I think of it as marital hazard.

Secondly, I ask myself if there is anything that I had vowed to do or not to do that I still find myself doing or not doing. Invariable, the answer is yes. So for example, each time I cleaned out my handbag, I would promise myself that I would not put so many things in the bag anymore. Well, let's just say my bag continues to have many "just-in-case-I-need-it" items.

Paul said in Romans 7: 1, *For the good that I would I do not: but the evil which I would not, that I do*. So my encouragement to you is, before you get off on some annoying habit of your spouse, apply the litmus test. Is it normal human behaviour?

55. Seek To Understand ♥

Try to understand men. If you understand each other, you will be kind to each other. John Steinbeck

Human beings are complex creatures. Full stop. (I am sure men will say women are more complex. But that's for another book). If we want to succeed in any relationship, we must seek to understand the other party. Before you jump to agree with me that your husband should seek to understand you, please remember that this letter is to you. Not your husband. You should therefore seek to understand him. And yes, he should seek to understand you too, but don't get side tracked. Let's focus on your part.

You have to actively seek to understand him.

This understanding is not a goal to be achieved, but a process to be engaged in. What am I saying? I do not believe that we can understand everything about a person. Additionally, we are constantly changing; constantly evolving. So, the seeking to understand has to be ongoing.

You will need to study him. For example, you need to learn if he is a morning or night person. Morning persons are up early, full of life and energy and eager to go. Night persons on the other hand, are full of energy during the night hours. I am sure you can clearly see how your relationship can be negatively impacted if you do not recognise when your husband functions best and adjust your expectations.

As I said before, we are all very complex beings and as such, we have to be actively engaged in seeking to understand our partners. The reality is, when we think we understand them, they change. As Lillian Hellman famously said, "People change and forget to tell each other." It is therefore up to us to develop the skill of recognising the changes and adjusting accordingly.

56. You Have All Of Him... Not Really ♥

People will only let their guard down, if they have no reason to keep it up. Unknown

When I was getting married, I remember the pastor asking in a very deliberate way, "Do you take Arnie Alfred Francis to be your lawful wedded husband?" He called Arnie's name slowly as if counting his words. Without hesitating, I gave a spritely, "I do" to which he replied, "You have all of him." The truth, however, is that a person rarely gives all of himself, all the time, to one person. There may be things that your spouse will not share with you for varied reasons. He may, however, share them with someone else.

Many women complain that their husbands do not share their thoughts or their inner most feelings. While that may be true, you must never make a fuss about it. In fact, if you do make a fuss, you are only giving your spouse more reason not to share with you.

You must accept that your spouse is 'a work in progress.' God is not through with him yet. Even if you are very, very close, there may be things that he may keep to himself for different reasons. Sometimes it may be a feeling of inadequacy. Most men are wired to think that they should be able to handle their problems by themselves. Some feel that they do not want to "burden" their spouse with their problems. For others, sharing causes embarrassment.

The best thing you can do is to be patient and create an atmosphere where he will feel comfortable to open up. If you sense that your husband is burdened about a matter, you can gently remind him that you are there for him. However, if he chooses not to share his burden, don't let it be an issue. The worst thing you can do is to nag him about his reluctance to talk. You should pray for him in earnest. Ask the Lord to release him from his burdens, to grant him wisdom to find a solution, to grant him favour, to give him instruction and direction. Never forget James 5:16, which tells us that *the prayer of a righteous person is powerful and effective*.

57. As Is! ♥

Acceptance of others brings an inner peace and tranquility instead of anger and resentment. Unknown

Steve Goodier said, "All of us have an invisible sign around our necks –"AS IS". It means take me as I am. I may not be what you want me to be, and I am far from perfect. But, I have some great qualities too. You will have to take me "as is" and I will take you that way too." (Edited) A long quote, which aptly captures the posture we should adapt with our spouse.

This may not be an easy thing to do. In fact, it is not even a natural thing to do. It is human nature to want to fix things perceived to be broken, but we are not things. We are complex human beings, who at times do not understand even our own selves. We do not even know what we will always do or say in any given situation

In Matthew 26:34, the Lord told Peter that he would deny Him three times before the cock crowed. Peter swore he wouldn't; but he did! God knows us more than we know ourselves! One of the most liberating positions to find oneself in is being able to let go of the things we cannot control. You cannot control your partner's behaviour. You can only control your actions and reactions.

You have to decide what behaviour you can accept and which you simply cannot live with. Before you jump to a conclusion, never forget that your partner is a package deal. You must weigh the negatives and the positives to reach a balanced position. Having considered all his attributes, and having made a decision to accept him 'as is' you must make peace with your decision. Do not allow it to be an issue. Focus on the positives and ask God's grace to assist you to deal with the negatives. When you do that, you will then be able to experience inner peace and tranquility instead of anger and resentment.

58. Just Let Him Be! ♥

The beginning of love is the will to let those we love be perfectly themselves. Thomas Merton

Successful people do what they ought to do; when they ought to do it; whether or not they feel like doing it. Since we want the best for our spouse, we may repeat the quote in an attempt to encourage him. However, there are times he will just not be in the mood to be encouraged. And it's not that he doesn't know what to do, but... So, if you lovingly remind him of what you think is important and warrants his attention and he does not respond; then let him be. Find knee city. Cry out to your God. Ask the Lord to nudge him. When the Lord does the nudging you do not get the blame for being a nag!

So for example, he has an important appointment for which he should prepare and he is watching television. After you mention (not instruct) that you think he should be preparing for the important appointment, let him be. Resist the temptation to 'pepper' him with instructions as to what he should be doing and when. The same principle applies to even his spiritual life. If you think that he is not reading his bible or praying enough: cry - no bawl - to God. Nagging your partner about doing what is right may result in resentment and resistance. He must come to the realisation on his own.

I know that this is not easy for some of us as we believe that it is our duty to prevent our spouse from messing up their lives. But we must never forget that we are all work-in-progress. Each of us is at a different stage in our spiritual, emotional or psychological development. We must therefore not expect our partner to think and act like us or even how we think that they should think and act.

One of the worst things you can do is communicate to your partner that he is not as successful as he could be because he doesn't do things the way you do or when you do them.

Sometimes you just have to let him be. But never cease to pray.

Ephesians 6:18 reminds us to *pray always with all prayer and supplication in the Spirit, and watching thereunto with all perseverance and supplication for all saints.*

59. Dealing With Mr. Popular ♥

Unrealistic expectations and poor communications can destroy any relationship. Unknown

Before marriage you may have loved the idea of dating someone popular. You may even have felt extra special when you became 'the one' now on the arms of Mr. Popular. But know that it is very likely he will continue to be popular after the wedding. When walking down the road or in the mall, do you have to stop umpteen times to greet the many persons that he knows or who know him?

How do you deal with the many interruptions? Rant, rave and misbehave? Surely not! You will have to ask yourself, "Was he popular before I married him; was this the norm?" Be honest and answer "Yes!" Then ask yourself, did I marry him knowing he was Mr. Popular? Be honest and answer, "Yes." Then send a silent prayer to your Lord for grace and patience to deal with the matter.

You can gently mention to your spouse that you long for some uninterrupted time with him because you love him and want him all to yourself. He may then decide to handle the interruptions differently but there is no guarantee he will. You must resist the temptation to bully him or curse him for being too friendly!

If any particular incident makes you uncomfortable, communicate your discomfort, but do not comment on the fact that he is 'popular.' After all, he may have little control over his popularity. So focus on maintaining a strong relationship with your husband.

Dealing with Mr. Popular usually requires patience, tolerance, God's grace and honest and gentle communication of your feelings to your partner. In addition, it is important that you remain confident in who you are and not allow his popularity to derail your confidence in any way.

Some wives complain that they feel as if people evaluate them to determine if they are fit to be the partner of Mr. Popular. My simple answer is that it really does not matter what the world and his wife think. An insightful quote credited to Eleanor Roosevelt states that, "No one can make you feel inferior without your consent." Never give anyone that permission.

Your duty is to focus on being the best Mrs. Right you can be and constantly pray for your marriage to withstand the many interruptions resulting from Mr. Popular's popularity.

60. Dealing With Mr. Cool ♥

Tolerance and celebration of individual differences is the fire that fuels lasting love. Tom Hannah

Many wives complain about their husband's lack of urgency concerning everything. They say that their husbands seem to dwell on "easy" street irrespective of the seriousness of a situation. Sometimes the husband will not even make the time to discuss the issues, much less to act on them.

This situation can be very frustrating for a wife. You must, however, resist the temptation to fly off the handle and curse him. This should not be an option for you. Please consider the warning in Psalms 109 vs. 17, *If you love to curse then curse shall come upon you and blessings shall be far from you.*

First pray. Ask the Lord to bring calm to your spirit. Ask for His guidance as to how, when and where to approach the subject with your partner. Your approach should respectfully communicate to your spouse that you understand that he has his way of dealing with things, which differs from yours. However, let him know your reasons for thinking the way you do and why you may deem his urgent response important at the time. He may be willing to listen or he may not be.

If he will not listen, then contemplate the worst-case scenario and decide if it is worth the tension in your marriage. Frankly, there may be times when you will suffer some loss. Loss of an opportunity, loss of money, or some other loss through the lethargy of your partner. If it happens, you must choose how you will react. Communicate your disappointment, but don't nag him with a million "I told you sos." Your words must be seasoned with grace (Colossians 4:6). You must seek God's grace to move on. Hopefully by your chaste conduct, you can win your husband over to be less lethargic. Never believe that bullying him will work. It will not. He will rebel and feel that you are trying to control him and dictate to him. This will only cause tension in your marriage.

The irony is that, if you are honest, you will admit that it was Mr. Cool's easy-going attitude, which swept you off your feet. So, since he may have had this attitude before marriage, you certainly shouldn't make it be an issue in the marriage. I encourage you to seek God's grace and His wisdom on how to deal with Mr. Cool.

61. Just Shut Up! ♥

Wise people are not always silent, but they know when to be. Unknown

It is a general rule that people do not like to be constantly told what to do. Neither do we enjoy being corrected. The problem, however, is that most, if not all women love to correct. Maybe it's our maternal instinct. But, it's a dangerous practice. It annoys our men. It is irrelevant that you are right! Your spouse will simply shut you out. You will lose him. In most cases when you are "correcting" you are criticising him in some way. I stated earlier, but will reiterate here, nothing sucks out the marrow out of the bone of a relationship like criticism. Sometimes you should just 'see and blind" and 'hear and deaf.' Bite your lip. Just shut up! It is not easy, but it will prove to be easier on the emotions than getting to a place in your relationship where you are talking and your spouse is right there, but just doesn't care to listen. It happens!

A story is told of a wife who insisted on 'correcting' her husband's driving. Every turn he made, she corrected him. Finally, he turned and simply asked her if she ever wondered how he managed to drive when she was not in the car... I recommend that sometimes when you see situations where your husband 'needs correction,' send up a silent prayer for him. Talk to God, but do not constantly criticize or nag. It usually does not achieve the desired effect.

Practice to overlook some things. Practice to just shut up!

62. Slewfoot's Door ♥

...Neither give place to the devil. Ephesians 4:27

A very animated Pentecostal preacher I know, always refers to Satan as slewfoot. I know there are other definitions and perspectives, but slewfoot is the word I have come to associate with Satan. I have also decided that irrespective of what happened in my marriage, I would not be the one to let slewfoot in. I decided that I would try very hard so that no one could point a finger at me, saying the breakdown in my marriage (if there should ever be one) is my fault. Now that is no easy feat to accomplish. In fact, it is not even a feat to be accomplished. It is an attitude to possess.

It is constantly telling yourself that you will choose NOT TO! Not to give in to the temptation to say unkind things. Not to keep malice. Not to do anything that will hurt, rather than build your marriage. Not to... Now this is easier said than done because slewfoot is so subtle that he will try to slip through any and everything. In a moment, in the twinkling of an eye, your spouse can do or say something that could conceivably change your spirit from fine to foul. At that time the enemy rushes in like a flood presenting you with various options you can undertake. It takes practice and more practice to not yield to his temptations. You have to develop the discerning eye to recognise when slewfoot is beckoning for a place in your life.

Let's not also forget that while man looketh on the outward, God knoweth the heart (1 Samuel 16:7). He knows the real motive why we do and say the things we do and say. We can't fool him. I have always felt that God will expose me as He knows the real me, so I might as well try my best to do right and not open the door for slewfoot. As tempting as it will be, I encourage you not to give slewfoot a place in your life. I encourage you to resolve not to be the door he uses to enter your marriage.

63. Be D.I.P ♥

True love doesn't happen by accident. It's deliberate, its intentional it's purposeful and in the end, it's worth it. Darlene Schacht

Be deliberate, intentional, purposeful (D.I.P). Marriage requires deliberate actions. You have to be intentional. You have to be purposeful. Marriage is a verb. A doing word. Marriage is work; day in, day out. There is no vacation. No day off. The more you invest in your marriage, the more you are likely to get out of it. Because the expression 'get married' is so common, persons go on to assume they also get the 'marriage.' But marriage is not something you get or get into. It's not something that is ready made. It is something that you and your spouse create.

Do what pleases your spouse as best as you can and as often as you can. Consistency is key. And consistency does not mean doing the same thing all the time. No. You must remember that we all change. Our tastes change; our preferences change. Sometimes even our dreams change. So we have to constantly seek to understand our partner to know how we can meet their changing needs.

You have to be deliberate about bringing energy to your marriage. Be deliberate about communicating. My husband and I try not to travel in the car in silence. We are very intentional about talking to each other. We chat about any and everything.

Even if it is the news of the day or sharing our plans for the day or sharing how our day went. Checking-in at least once during the day is also a good practice. With technology, there are so many ways to keep in touch. Nothing is nicer than receiving a message of love: An "Are you OK?" note says, "I am thinking about you and I do care how you are doing."

Be intentional about creating a warm atmosphere - one which invites your husband to hurry home. Just think that every negative utterance will create a dark, ominous cloud in your home, while every positive one will bring light and sunshine. Remember Proverbs 18:21 says, *There is death and life in the power of the tongue.* So the words you speak will either breathe more life into your marriage or slowly kill it.

Laughter cements marriages. Develop the habit of making your spouse laugh. Even if it's at your expense! Study him to know what will make him laugh. Remember the popular saying; laughter is the best medicine. (Of course they also say if you laugh for no reason, you need medicine. But that's an entirely different story)!

64. Wow Him! ♥

Happiness lies in the joy of achievement and the thrill of creative effort. Franklin D. Roosevelt

Nothing adds spice to a relationship like the element of surprise. Be creative. Think outside the box. Do things that your partner would not expect, but will certainly find delightful. During courtship, we ladies sometimes went to great lengths to impress our then not-yet-husbands. After the wedding, we should continue to make every effort to impress our now lawfully-wedded-husbands.

I started to write poems to my husband early in our marriage. Not only did it amaze him, it amazed me too, because I did not even like to write! One of the poems I wrote was:

I Love Sharing Space With You

I love sharing space with you
I love being in any place with you
I love seeing your face in any place
I just love sharing space with you

Whether it's in the car
Or we are walking up the hill very far

Or maybe it's under a tree
As long as it's you and me
The feeling holds true
I love sharing space with you

There's a certain magic in your presence
I think it must be God-sent
Cause when I'm with you
I feel so loved, so treasured, so secured too
I just love sharing space with you

You have been my soul mate
For nigh two decades
I believe our love was heaven-made
I can be the real me when I am with you

I just love sharing space with you.

You may not write poems, but maybe you could sing to him or dance for him or plan a special day for him.

I remember once before one of Arnie's birthday, I emailed him a detailed programme (hour by hour) of activities for his birthday. It included breakfast in bed (not food), going to the beach, a full body massage (by me), a pedicure, a nap, going out for dinner then dessert in bed (not food). He was wowed! In fact, for days after, he kept talking about the day. He couldn't believe that I had managed to fit in so many activities in one day.

The idea is to be creative and do something that is "just for him." With a little thought, you can come up with something that can blow his mind. (Hopefully not literally!)

65. Doing "I'm Sorry"

Believe what you see and forget what you heard. Unknown

Many women complain that their husbands never express regret for anything - that they never say, "I'm sorry." However, some of these same women confess that they know that their husbands do regret their actions. Their husbands will not say they are sorry but will "do" they are sorry. These women can decide whether to accept the fact that their spouse is indeed sorry and move on, or prolong the tension in the marital relationship because their husbands refuse to SAY they are sorry.

To some, it's a no-brainer; action speaks louder than words. Others hold on to their hurt because they have not HEARD the words, "I'm sorry." I believe this is another case where it is wise to do a cost-benefit analysis. Determine if it is worth the tension, stress and lack of intimacy in your relationship even though you are convinced that your spouse is indeed sorry, but just will not verbally express that regret.

We will not receive everything we desire in life. So while it is desirable to hear the words, we have to make a choice to protect our marriage from decay if our spouse is not willing to say, but will "do" I'm sorry.

Of course, if he makes it a habit to repeat "mistakes", then whether he says he's sorry or "Does I'm Sorry", he may not be sorry after all. He may be sick. Either way, your marriage needs professional help.

66. PMS Is Real ♥

Just because your pain is understandable, doesn't mean your behaviour is acceptable. Steve Maraboli

Many women suffer from some degree of premenstrual syndrome (PMS) during their lifetime. Many, however, are not conscious when this is happening. PMS symptoms occur between ovulation and the start of the period. It is well documented that the symptoms of PMS include headaches, bloating, fatigue, cramps, depression, mood swings, irritability, low sex drive, sadness, lack of energy, amongst others.

You ought to know your body well enough so you are aware of its changes. While your symptoms are very real, they should provide no excuse to unleash your fury on your spouse. I once listened to a sermon from Pastor Hagee in which he said, "The only difference between a snarling dog and a woman during PMS, is lipstick!" Of course, the remark evoked laughter from his audience, but the sad truth is that some women's behaviour during PMS is no laughing matter.

Being aware of your body and its changes should enable you to take steps to reduce the impact of PMS.

While some men are very sensitive or knowledgeable and realise that you are experiencing PMS, some have no clue. You cannot therefore expect him to know that it is PMS time; hence stay clear of you. Talk to him; even if you do not feel like talking. Still talk - even if it is just to ask him for some alone time while you deal with your challenges. But he should at least be aware of what you are going through. Your marriage is too important for you to allow anything to cause a disconnect between you and your spouse. You have to be vigilant. You have to be alert. As soon as you recognise that a matter could cause an issue, deal with it. Do not sweep it under the carpet.

So while PMS is real, you can decide that you will be proactive and take steps to reduce the negative impact it can have on your marriage. Others have done it and so can you.

67. The Big "M" Word ♥

Change your thinking and it will change your life. Unknown

As a young woman contemplating marriage, I saw a pamphlet with a middle-aged woman in a long night-gown looking through a window. She looked forlorn. Her husband was standing behind her with his hand on her shoulder; the same forlorn look on his face.

The pamphlet was about menopause and stated amongst other things that it could affect your sex life. I remember saying to myself, "No wonder the husband looks forlorn. He was getting no sex!" I decided there and then, if I got married and was blessed to reach middle age, I would do everything in my power to protect my sex life. I certainly would not be wearing anything that looked like that long nightgown I saw the woman wearing on the pamphlet!

So ladies, menopause is real. There is no doubt about that. If you have experienced or are experiencing that phase of your life, you probably are experiencing some negative effects. But I encourage you not to simply roll over and play dead. Make a decision to minimise, if not eliminate the negative effects of menopause on your life.

There is much available information about diet and exercise which can reduce the effects of menopause. Be proactive. Take charge. If not, you may find that menopause consumes you and your marriage. You may have no interest in sex during this time. You may be depressed and not even be aware that you are depressed. You may not want your husband to touch you or even be near you.

Menopause can last between two and ten years! If you are not proactive, then this period of your life may very well be like a roller coaster ride. You have to be deliberate. You cannot just give in to your feelings. Share these changes with your spouse. Do everything in your power to protect the intimacy in your marriage. OK, so what if there was no intimacy before menopause? Well that's a whole different story for another letter!

68. Enough Of The Pretense! ♥

A bizarre sensation pervades a relationship of pretense. No truth seems true. Maya Angelou

I am not sure if it is a woman's thing or a certain-type-of-people's thing. But some people actually subscribe to malingering or simply just pretending they feel worse than they really do. Many women pretend to be sick to see how their partner will treat them. It is a ploy for attention. The degree of love and attention they receive while being "sick" will be viewed as the extent or quality of their partner's love for them.

I believe this is a dangerous practice. It is manipulation. No matter how much your husband loves you, it is likely to add some pressure or stress to him when you are not well. It is that simple. It is not a good practice to either pretend to be ill or exaggerate illness. It could backfire. Be honest about your situation and do not exaggerate or use it to get out of some responsibility. The Lord requires that *we lead a quiet and peaceable life in all godliness and honesty* (1Timothy 2:2).

When you pretend, you run the risk of falling prey to the 'wolf-wolf' trap. When you are genuinely ill and need attention, you may be ignored. I have been told by some women that their husbands are cold because they do not give them any attention when they are ill. But in the same breath, some of them will say that they had in the past pretended to be ill to see how he would react. That action will erode trust and destroy your relationship. So enough of the pretense!

69. He-brews ♥

By wisdom a house is built, and by understanding it is established.
Proverbs 24:3

A wife and husband were arguing about domestic chores. The husband stated it was the wife's duty to get up and make breakfast. The wife disagreed. Her support? - The bible. She declared that a book in the bible believed to be written by Paul says, "He brews!" That means, he is responsible for "brewing" the coffee and thus he should make the breakfast. "A suh mi get it, a suh mi sell it." (Translated: I am repeating a story the same way I heard it). I doubt that wife was a Jamaican, but I will not hazard a guess as to her nationality.

The difference in the perspectives as to the role of the husband and wife in performing domestic chores is the source of many marital conflicts. In most cases, the perspectives are by-products of their respective upbringing. If the husband never sees his father involved in domestic chores, then he will more likely than not believe that domestic chores is a "woman thing." On the other hand, if he saw his father or other respected male figure(s) involved in doing chores, then it is likely that he will not have a problem doing chores.

This is a significant area of a couple's domestic affairs to be agreed on before marriage. Each person's expectations should be clearly articulated. If they can't agree on who will do what, then the wedding should be delayed until they can agree!

What if you were so in love that the mundane discussion about who will cook or do dishes just never entered your thoughts? What if you are now being told that there is an expectation that household chores are the purview of the wife? And now that the wedding is over and the marriage has begun, there is conflict?

I suggest you try to lovingly discuss the positive impact his participation in the household chores would have on the marriage. Of course the very obvious, is that you would have more time for him!

Please note I said, "lovingly discuss..." I know you might be rolling your eyes thinking that you should not have to discuss this. You may be thinking that he lives in the house and is a beneficiary of the chores and as such it should be logical that he participates. Dale Carnegie says we need to remember when dealing with people, we are not dealing with creatures of logic, but creatures of emotion.

So while you may think it's logical for him to participate in chores, he may not think so. The key is to reach a position where both persons are comfortable. You may need to get professional help to settle the conflict if you two cannot settle it.

70. This Matter Of Money ♥

Money can't buy love, but fighting about it will bankrupt your relationship. Michelle Singletary

Money is a major source of conflict in relationships. Whether it is the lack of money, whose it is or how it is used, money causes problems. It is my view that many of those conflicts are avoidable if we accept our partner's money personality.

This does not happen, however, as many of us simply cannot tolerate anyone who does not share our views on money. A saver will most likely think of a spender as careless. A spender may consider a saver a cheapskate or mean.

You should strive to reach a position of acceptance. Accept that your spouse's view on money is very different from yours. Have very frank and open discussions about each other's money personality. Such discussions should be devoid of attacks and should instead seek to understand the other person's point of view.

Now in my mind, the ideal position is that a couple maintains joint accounts into which all income is lodged. Then they both sit down (or stand up) and agree on how every single cent should be spent. Once the agreements are lived up to, there would then be absolutely no problem at all in this area.

Well, there is the ideal and the real deal. The real deal is that couples rarely see eye to eye on how money should be spent. This makes it a very high risk area for conflict.

As with any other area of conflict in the relationship, my approach is 'reach common ground.' When there is mutual respect in the relationship, even when there are differences there is always a willingness to reach common ground. Common ground is what works for both of you.

So it may be that you decide on having separate accounts with each party responsible for certain bills or a certain percentage of all bills. Or if you maintain a joint account you could agree on a monthly allowance that each person can spend without having to provide an account for.

Like any other problem in a marriage, its resolution will depend on your attitude. If you display a high-handed approach then the conflicts will continue. If you are always nagging your spouse about spending habits, then the conflicts will continue. You must resist the temptation to nag and nag. (Even one nag is not good!)

Your attitude must communicate a willingness to respect (even if you disagree with) your partner's attitude towards money. With such an attitude, you have a greater chance of resolving the money conflicts which may arise in your marriage. Ralph Waldo Emerson once said, "Money costs too much."

As I read the quote, I had to agree. In so many cases, money costs us our joy, our peace of mind, our health, our relationships, our lives! Fighting about money could cost you your marriage. Is it really worth it?

71. Yes Dear ♥

Love seeketh not her own. 1 Corinthians 13:5

Someone once said, "A happy wife makes a happy life." So some men encourage other men to simply agree with their wives for a peaceful life. I would like to suggest that if your husband agrees with everything you say, then something is wrong - very wrong. It could be that he cannot be bothered to disagree with you because he knows what will ensue. So he simply says, "Yes dear."

Then again, some women curse their spouse for their 'yes dear' attitude. So the poor man is left confused. If he disagrees with his wife, it brings an argument, if he agrees it brings an argument because he never has anything to say! He may think, "I'm damned if I do and damned if I don't," so will simply choose the path of least resistance.

Just know that while you may get your way, you may end up creating an environment that robs your marriage of valuable, objective input from your spouse. Men and women are wired to think differently. (I know you may be tempted to inject that men just do not think, but I will not go there).

Your posture must communicate to your spouse that you value his input; you want to hear what he has to say; it is important to you what he thinks. If he continually hears that he has no sense, then he will think, 'Why bother?'

The next time your spouse responds, "Yes dear" pause and evaluate your actions and attitude. Pay attention to his attitude; his body language, his tone of voice. It could be that he had decided that if he proffered an opinion it will not be accepted anyway. So he simply says, "Yes dear."

72. Leave You Alone. Really? ♥

Let no corrupt communication proceed out of your mouth.
Ephesians 4:29

It is the practice of many women to "run" their men as soon as there is a disagreement. They make it a habit to say to their husbands, "Why don't you leave me alone?" Some husbands do just that - permanently! They simply pack their things and leave the home - never to return. While I do not have the statistics, I have met several women who regret losing their husbands in this way. I encourage you not to practice to tell your husband to leave you alone. You may just get your wish.

Except in extreme cases including physical and mental abuse, most women who lose their husbands, if honest, will confess that they miss them. While the husbands were at home, these wives focused on their negative attributes. However, when they left, somehow their minds remembered only the positives. It is wise to learn from the mistakes of others.

Accept the fact that your husband is imperfect and he may possess traits that will annoy the "heaven" out of you. You must however refrain from telling him to leave you alone - because he might do just that!

73. Watch Your Report ♥

So then every one of us shall give account of himself to God.
Romans 14:12

I heard a story about a wife who called her mother and asked if she could stay with her. She'd had enough of her marriage and was calling it quits. The mother tried to encourage her to stay. However, the wife was adamant that she was through! She reeled off all her husband's faults that were driving her crazy. Her mother agreed to allow her stay awhile.

On her arrival, her mother gave her a piece of paper and before she could say anything the wife said, "Mother I know you are going to say that I should list all my husband's good points and then list all his faults." Her mother replied, "Not quite, my dear. I want you to draw a line down the middle of the paper. On the left, write all your husband's annoying habits. When you are through, write your reaction to each of those annoying habits on the right side of the paper."

When she was through, the wise mother took the paper, tore it down the middle and gave the fed up wife the side of paper with her reactions. As she read each line, she welled up in tears as she recognised how unkind and sometimes even cruel she had been to her husband.

I know it's easy to cite cause and effect, that is, to say the actions of her husband caused her to react the way she did. But we are responsible for our actions. We cannot control the actions of our spouse but how we react is entirely up to us. Someone once said that our reaction to a situation has the power to change the situation itself. Again, it takes great self-control and grace from God to act appropriately at all times. What will your report look like?

74. Refuse To Live in Bondage ♥
Emancipate yourself from mental slavery. Bob Marley

Your partner will do and say things that will hurt you. Sometimes it is even done intentionally. The choice is yours to either store up the hurt or to let it go. If you choose to store it up, you are actually choosing to live in bondage, that is, to be held captive by the hurt and pain. Invariably you also put your marriage in bondage. The stored hurt and pain will cause you to be hostile or at best, cold towards your partner. Your partner too finds himself in prison; being held captive by a hostile and tension filled atmosphere.

You must choose to forgive. One author says forgiveness is giving up your right to hurt the other person for hurting you. That's not easy. You will need time to get over the pain of being hurt but communicate this need for a "time-out" to your partner. Say to him, "You have hurt me in this way and I need some time to heal." You also need to ask God to help you with the healing process and not store up the hurt. The 'cancer' of unforgiveness will transform you into an aggressive beast. You will become unbearable, existing in an unhealthy marriage.

Find a trusted friend or a Christian counsellor and share your hurt. Do what you have to do, but doing nothing and embracing the hurt should not be an option. You must refuse to live in bondage.

75. Relationship Plaque ♥

Bitterness is a result of clinging to negative experiences.
Leon Brown

Every now and again when I flash my pearly whites (ok, maybe not so white), I see a build up of some whitish matter at the base. That build-up I've learned, is called plaque. Plaque is a sticky film that contains millions of bacteria and builds on your teeth if not diligently removed. The bacteria in plaque causes tooth decay and gum disease. I'm sure you see where I'm going with this...

Your relationship will suffer decay if you do not remove the "plaque" from it. I believe the single most significant factor which leads to relationship plaque is unforgiveness. I will not pretend that forgiveness is easy. But I believe if you keep Matthew 6:14-15 at the front of your mind it will make the process easier. That scripture says, *For if you forgive men when they sin against you, your heavenly father will also forgive you. But if you do not forgive men their sins, your Father will not forgive your sins.*

So you have a vested interest in forgiving. Forgiving your spouse is not so much about your spouse as it is about you.

Other issues which may cause plaque build up in your relationship are malice, the non-acceptance of your spouse and unrealistic expectations.

Relationship plaque prevents the relationship from "breathing." It disrupts communication and causes tension. It is said that prevention is better than cure, so I encourage you to be very alert to the circumstances that will cause plaque to build up.

Ephesians 4:27 says, *Neither give place to the devil*. When we refuse to deal with the issues which are negatively affecting our marriage, we are giving place to the devil. So I encourage you, as much as is dependent on you, deal quickly with the issues, which if left unresolved could cause "relationship plaque."

76. Tell Him! ♥

Perhaps you will forget the kind words you say today, but the recipient may cherish them over a lifetime. Dale Carnegie

I am assuming that your husband possesses some qualities that you like. Does he know or merely suspects? Quite often, we think about these things but never express them. I encourage you to tell your husband what you like about him. And yes, I know your husband may not tell you what he likes about you. But is that a reason not to express what may be inside your heart? The enemy will say, "Yes!" You will even feel justified in not saying anything since your husband does not say anything either. However, you must remember that is how Satan works. He prefers to build walls instead of bridges.

When you say what you like about your husband, it is a reflection of who you are and not who he is. You are expressing how you feel, what truly gives you pleasure. Make sure that your motive is pure. If you are simply fishing for a return compliment and it is not forthcoming, you will feel hurt.

Saying something nice may feel unnatural or uncomfortable if it is not something that you normally do. You may even sound fake at first, but over time, it will feel more natural.

Think back to the days when you could not wait to tell a friend about all the things you liked about "this guy." Well, "this guy" is now yours! Tell him what you would have told your friend.

Like his smell? Tell him. How about the way he dresses? Hmmm. His manly or teddy-bear-like physique is just what the doctor ordered? Tell him! You may like his caring, sensitive and understanding personality. If you like how he sings or prays or worships the Lord, tell him. Whatever it is, tell him!

77. A Working Penis ♥

It's not happy people who are thankful,
its thankful people who are happy. Unknown

The office can be extremely stressful. If we are not careful, we will not enjoy life but be consumed daily by stress of some sort. There may be tight deadlines, inadequate resources, demanding clients, staff issues - and the list goes on and on. It is enough to cause you to sink in depression. Sometime ago, I felt a cloud of depression descending to engulf me. Fortunately, the words of the song, "Count your blessings, name them one by one and it would surprise you what the Lord has done," came to mind.

So I started to give thanks for every working part of my body. I don't think I was able to think of all the body parts, nonetheless, I started to name the major parts - my eyes, my hands, my feet, my liver, my lungs, my kidney, my heart, my mouth....

Then I said to myself, I need to give thanks for the working parts of my husband also. I was not at the doctor's office with him after all. That was a lot to give thanks for. So I started to give God thanks for his eyes, his hands, his feet, his mouth, his kidney, his heart. Then I remembered his penis! My spirit immediately lifted and I broke out in a wide grin. I really thanked the Lord for my husband's working penis. I remembered not only numerous times of pleasure, but my two wonderful sons that working penis produced. After that thought, I was energised to face the challenges before me.

I encourage you to give God thanks every day for your husband. Name all his positive attributes and give thanks. Give thanks too for all his working body parts. And if you are like me you will give thanks for his working penis!

78. Build Memories ♥

Happy memories become treasures in the heart to pull out on the tough days. Charlotte Kasi

If you are blessed with long life together, every now and again you will look back on the journey of your life. You will ruminate on the things you did. You will recount the places you went. The reminiscing will evoke some kind of emotion. Ensure that you engage in activities that you both enjoy.

There is a joke (well, it must be a joke) that an elderly man was asked what was the secret to his long lasting marriage. He responded that he and his wife went dinner and dancing twice per week. He went on Tuesdays and Thursdays and she went on Wednesdays and Fridays.

It is not uncommon for women to pretend that they enjoy certain activities (such as cricket or basketball) during courtship, but would not be caught dead going to a game or even watching it with their husbands. I am suggesting that if you used to pretend to enjoy an activity, please continue to pretend until you truly like it. Couples must share time and space in a relaxing manner. Either you plan activities (if you are the planner) or ensure that you agree to participate in activities suggested by your partner.

They don't have to be elaborate. A simple beach trip or a road trip is a start. However, it must be planned, agreed on and committed to. If you are the more serious one, you may be tempted to trivialize the need to 'waste' money in this manner. On the contrary, fun activities done together, can add zest to your marriage. A friend of mine once told me that she was the designated entertainment coordinator in her family. Her role was to plan activities that the whole family could participate in and enjoy.

Many wives complain that their husbands lack creativity and if they do not suggest that they do something together, nothing happens. My response is, "Can you imagine if the eyes said to the ear, I am tired of doing the seeing, why can't you do it sometimes?"

Galatians 6:9 exhorts, *Be not weary in well doing*. Resist the temptation to cease to plan activities, simply because you are always the one doing the planning. When you are tired of planning, rest, then start again.

I encourage you to create memories - and not just memories - but beautiful memories. Memories that will evoke laughter, gratitude and warmth as you look back over the years.

79. Nip It In The Bud ♥

A wise man feareth, and departeth from evil: but the fool rageth, and is confident. Proverbs 14:16

I often receive complaints from wives that their husbands are not affectionate, sensitive or caring. And sometimes the enemy allows Mr. Affectionate, Mr. Sensitive or Mr. Caring to cross our path. And not just to cross our path, but to stop in our path and give us the very attention we have been longing for. Just the way we like it. In the right proportion. At the right time and the right place! He may be a co-worker, a neighbour or a church brother. A friendship is struck quite harmlessly. Casual check-ins grow to daily check-ins and before you know it, emotional adultery sets in.

Never for one moment think that you are so strong, so spirit-filled, so water-baptized, so speaking-in-tongues that the enemy cannot trap you. Not only can he entrap you, he will devour you! 1 Peter 5:8 tells us to, *Be sober, be vigilant, because the adversary the devil, as a roaring lion, walketh about, seeking whom he may devour.*

God knows why through His word, He warns us to be vigilant!

When you feel the urge or the need to speak to a man, be in his company, share every detail of your life and you tell yourself "he is just a friend," you are in trouble. Big trouble! The enemy has lined you up for a bull's eye attack. Nip it in the bud! Stop! Just stop! Force yourself to stop the check-ins. Stop discussing you. Just stop! Believe me, when you feel drawn to someone that way, it's only a matter of time before disaster strikes.

Be honest with yourself. If you are emotionally attached to "a friend" in a way that you should be to your husband, seek help. It's not a good place to be. Find someone you can confide in or a Christian counsellor outside your circle and let them help you. You need help. If you keep telling yourself that the relationship is harmless, you will end up destroying your marriage. Believe me!

80. If You Stray ♥
The way of the transgressor is hard. Proverbs 13:15

I hardly believe that a wife would respond in the affirmative if asked if she would cheat on her husband. Well maybe I should say a Christian wife! I am aware that there are women who would not think twice about cheating.

However the fact that we are sinners saved by grace means that our sinful nature is still within us. And it is a known fact that Christian wives do fall by the wayside too. As I have said in previous letters, I believe that as soon as a minister pronounces a man and a woman, husband and wife, Satan assigns an imp to destroy that marriage. I have held that view as a young believer and now that I am, hmm... not old, but older, I still believe it. In fact, I have seen so many failed marriages in the church that my belief has been strengthened.

So if the unthinkable happens and you stray, you first must seek forgiveness from your heavenly father. The word of God says in 1 John 1:9, *If we confess our sins, he is faithful and just to forgive us our sins, and to cleanse us from all unrighteousness.*

Of course, you will then move on to seek forgiveness from your spouse. This is where I now hasten to caution, your spouse is not God. As much as it is desirable that he forgives you, he may simply not be able to. That's just the plain truth. The fact that he may not forgive you is between him and his God. He will be the one that will not be able to get forgiveness from God. You on the other hand, can only demonstrate true repentance and pray that God will give him the grace to forgive you. You cannot be the one to dictate the timeline in which he should "get over it." People heal at different paces.

Since trust has been broken, you have to be prepared to be mistrusted. He may become suspicious of your every move. However, I am old enough - no, let's rephrase that, I have lived long enough, to see marriages restored after trust has been broken. Continue to do the things that will demonstrate that the betrayal will not be repeated and exercise patience with your spouse. It will not be easy to regain trust, but it's not impossible.

81. The Big 'S' Word ♥

The wife's submission is not a matter of superior versus inferior; rather, it is self-imposed as a matter of obedience to the Lord and of love for her husband. Steve Pearce

Ephesians 5:22 says, *Wives submit yourself to your own husbands*. This verse invariably evokes a defensive spirit in most women; even in the very godly. The concept of submission does not sit well with most of us. I have heard many women scoff at the idea of submitting to their husbands. As far as they are concerned, he has no sense (look who he married!).

However my response to them is this: never forget that the instruction in Ephesians 5:22 is not from your husband; it is from God. And it is no different from the other instructions given to us either as children of God, joint heirs with Christ or godly wives. It is no different from the instruction in Matthew 5:44, *Love your enemies*; or in Philippians 2:3, *Let each esteem the other better than themselves*, or Hebrews 13:17, *Obey those who have authority over you*.

I have come to realize that we have no problem with submission if we agree with the instruction given to us (even though some of us simply hate being told what to do. Can I get an amen?) The issue arises when we disagree with the instructions or requests made of us. When these situations arise, we therefore need to draw on our approach in dealing with disagreements.

It would also help to remember Ephesians 5:21, *Submit yourselves one to another...* The bible expects mutual submission. So verse 22 is not the first request to submit.

The model for perfect submission was demonstrated by our Lord on several occasions. The bible recounts one instance in which He prayed three times asking His Father if it be possible to let the cup (dying on the cross) be passed from Him." Nevertheless, not my will but thine be done," he concluded. I believe that these eight words are the model for submission. (Nevertheless not my will, but thine be done.) Submission is not about being a doormat or allowing your spouse to make all the decisions without your input. It is about submitting your will to the will of God. It is accepting the biblical principle that God has set the man to lead. It is about respecting your spouse and communicating to him in your attitude that you are a godly woman, who is willing to adhere to biblical principles.

In a loving relationship where there is mutual respect, the husband is likely to consult with his wife when making decisions which affect them both. The success of the marriage is a team effort, so it is likely that a smart husband will rely on his wife in areas where she is stronger. That is not relinquishing his leadership role: in fact, on the contrary. When the marriage succeeds, he looks good!

I do not think that a wife should be resentful of the idea of submission, especially when she understands that submission goes both ways (see Ephesians 5:21). I believe that the enemy has sullied the word submission and has caused it to evoke negative emotions in women. However, in loving relationships where both parties are doing their best to adhere to the word of God, submission is a non-issue as there is mutual submission.

82. How Is My Wife-ing? ♥

*We all need people who will give us feedback.
That is how we improve. Bill Gates*

I have seen the sign *How is my driving?* on a number of vehicles. I am convinced that based on the actions of some of these drivers, they either do not know that the sign is there, they do not remember or they simply couldn't care less!

I am suggesting that at regular intervals you should have a heart to heart talk with your partner concerning how you are performing as a wife. I know this takes courage as we are giving our partner permission to criticize us. No one really likes criticism. However, I believe if this is done in an open and respectful way, it can only do your marriage good.

Arnie and I normally have this 'review' on our wedding anniversary. We give each other feedback on how we can best meet each other's needs. That is what the marriage is about - meeting each other's needs in a way that will bring honour and glory to God. So we may have to ask outright, what can I do to make you feel more loved, appreciated? Very few couples bother to do this review as they generally know what they are not doing to please their partners.

But whether your husband is at the place to reciprocate the question or not, that should not stop you from asking him. If you bear in mind that you are serving your husband *as unto the Lord* (Colossians 3:23) then you should be concerned about what God thinks about your service to your husband.

So ask your husband, how is your "wife-ing" and when he responds with any shortcomings, resist being defensive. It will take great humility, especially as many of us believe we are doing the best we can. However, this is another way you can communicate your love for your husband by being willing to be open and to address any shortcomings he may identify.

83. Love Him His Way ♥

We must first learn what is important to our spouse.
Gary Chapman

Many women have theories about how they will love their husbands when they get married. These theories are often influenced by their upbringing, their culture or maybe some instructions given to them by older, trusted women.

As a teenager, I had gone to the hairdresser and a heated discussion on men and women relationships had flared up. I listened intently but had nothing to contribute to the discussion. How could I? I was only a teenager.

However, as the hairdresser bent over me scrubbing my sore scalp, she said, "Young gyal, when yuh get big, you mus' know how to hold yuh man."(English translation: Young girl when you become an adult, you must know how to keep your man). Based on the instructions which followed, my puerile mind realised that she was not talking about how to hold his hands or hug him, but how to keep him interested in me at all times. How to keep him happy. How to keep his love tank full.

Get to know your husband and do not expect every cliché to apply to him. So for example, you may be inclined to spend a lot of time in the kitchen cooking up a storm to make a big spread for him. After all, you have heard that the way to a man's heart is through his stomach. And you want to please him. However, maybe he would be satisfied with a simple meal (sometimes no meal at all) and more love making or just some quality time rubbing his heads. (Yes, the plural is deliberate!)

You may love to see your home neat and tidy (as most women do) but that may not be as important to him as say, going out together.

The point I am making is that sometimes you may have to turn off the stove, or delay the house cleaning for some time so that you can do something he wants do. Simply put...so that you can love him, his way.

84. Be Alert! ♥

Watch ye, stand fast in the faith, quit you like men, be strong. 1 Corinthians 16:13

I understand that a young lady went home from church really excited and told her friends that she had met the man of her dreams. She said he was handsome, warm, seemed loving and caring. As her friends got excited at her wonderful news, she continued, "there is a little hurdle though, his wife goes to the same church!"

If I were not married, then maybe I would have found the story funny. But I think marriage is a very, very serious matter. So I cannot partake in even seemingly harmless jokes about an illicit involvement with a married man. As a wife, you must be alert to the fact that some women simply do not respect the marital status of your husband. In fact, some are positively challenged by it.

They will misquote Psalms 23, "The Lord is my shepherd, I see what I want."

They will go after your husband and brazenly tell you that you can keep the ring but they want the man! Be alert to the possibility of losing your husband to another woman. Yes, I know, he may be a Holy-Ghost-filled, water-baptised,

Jesus-on-his-mind kind of a husband. But trust me, each person has an Achilles' heel and the enemy will strategize to find it.

If you think that your husband is too close to another female, let him know how the relationship affects you. Do not accuse him of having an extra marital affair (unless you have solid evidence). Never nag him. That is the worst thing you could do! Just communicate to him how you feel. As hard as it may be, swallow all your pride and ask if that person may be filling a need that you are not. Maybe that person will listen to him, while you are always correcting, criticising or instructing him.

You also need to present that relationship to the Lord through prayer and fasting. If you have prayer partners that you trust, you can enlist their help to avert the potential danger. Never feel so comfortable in your marriage that you take it for granted. Know that your marriage is always under spiritual attack. Ephesians 6:12 tells us, *We wrestle not against flesh and blood but against principalities, against powers, against the rulers of darkness of this world, against spiritual wickedness in high places*. I have seen seemingly rock solid marriages broken into pieces. No marriage is immune to the attack of the enemy. Get on the offensive. Be alert!

85. Too Close For Comfort ♥

Anger cancels good judgement. Sister Souljah

Your spouse may be one of those very nice guys who has many female friends and confidantes. Or he could have one "special" one. Many sisters seek his counsel or even his attention and he may see absolutely nothing wrong with that. Indeed on the face of it, nothing is wrong. But as wives, we may feel very uncomfortable if we believe that a particular sister is getting too much of our partner's attention. I have listened to many wives complain that their husbands will be at the beck and call of church sisters, but she is unable to get him to respond to her requests. Equally, I have listened to husbands who say they cannot see why their wives are making an issue out of an innocent relationship. In fact, some men claim that they are displaying Christian qualities by being nice to other sisters. And they fail to understand why their wives are fussing over what they consider a non-issue.

My dear, this is a very delicate matter. Let me explain. If you fuss about how close he is to a particular sister and you keeping nagging him, that sister may just become more attractive to him. Why? She is not nagging him! She may be unloading her problems on him and he may be providing a shoulder (not necessarily literally) for her to cry on. Most men like to feel like they are problem solvers. In fact, some will boast that they are solution-oriented. So, they feel fulfilled, accomplished, valued and appreciated when a sister or sisters rely on them for advice and comfort. On the contrary, their wives spend more time correcting them and reminding them of their shortcomings. So while you may believe that nagging your spouse about his too-close relationship with a sister, or any other woman for that matter, will bring him closer to you, the very opposite usually happens. And therein lies the problem!

One thing is certain nagging your husband about his attachment to another woman will not make him more drawn to you.

Your burning question now is, "So what do I do?" There is no 'one-size-fits-all' response. It depends. It depends on the relationship you have with your husband. It depends on his temperament. It depends on...

Remain calm and do not think of the worst. Stop thinking that this "home-wrecker" is going to destroy your marriage. Remember, you are the one still living at home with your husband. Always pray before raising the issue with your husband. If you must share your concern with someone, make sure the person is responsible, trustworthy and able to offer sound advice. Praying must always be your first response, not your last resort.

Mark 1:35 says *Jesus rose while it was still dark and prayed*. It would be wise to follow that example.

You are in warfare. You must always be in a spiritual combative mode. Not against your husband, but against anything or anyone who seeks to come against your marriage intentionally or otherwise.

You should discuss with your spouse how uncomfortable you are with his actions. Remember your tone is important. It should not be an accusatory tone. One writer said that ten percent of conflicts is due to difference in opinion and ninety percent is due to wrong tone of voice.

In addition, use your feminine skill to regain your husband's attention. Nagging will not do it. I repeat; nagging will not do it!

86. If He Strays ♥

Unforgiveness is choosing to stay trapped in a jail cell of bitterness, serving time for someone's crime. Unknown

The very thought of your husband being unfaithful is repulsive. When you were getting married, this was the last thing on your mind. Although, if some women dared to be honest, even when they are saying "I do" there was an unease deep down in their stomachs. They knew even then that their husbands were likely to cheat on them. But they went through with the rites and soon enough they had to face the reality of an unfaithful husband.

So what next? Almost all the letters before would have – in one way or another – been preparing you for this awful moment. You must collect yourself and ask some hard questions. Is it possible that you might have pushed him into the arms of another woman? That does not excuse him, but it may help you to understand the reason. Can you find it in your heart to forgive him? Are you prepared for the consequences of a divorce? None of these questions should be answered hastily. You should take your time to answer them honestly. Talk with a born again counsellor who can show you different perspectives and the consequences of any decision taken.

How you relate to your spouse may depend on his attitude. He may be penitent or defensive. If he shows sincere regret but you simply cannot accept it, you must let him know. But I encourage you to resist the natural tendency to be bitter. This is definitely more easily said than done, but the truth is, bitterness hurts you more. It robs you of your joy and peace and the result is a toxic relationship in which no resolution can be reached.

If you truly cannot forgive, you must make peace with the decision to end your marriage. On the other hand, you may forgive him but still choose to end your marriage. In this case you have decided that while you forgive him, you are not willing to risk being hurt in this way again. That's your prerogative. But if you choose not to end the marriage you must also choose to forgive him and return to "normalcy" in the relationship. Living constantly in an acrimonious atmosphere is simply not an option. You were not created to live that way. In fact that is not living!

You also cannot decide to stay in the marriage and refuse your husband sex. That is not a marriage. Sex to a marriage is what fuel is to a car. Unless one party is ill or both parties agree to abstain due to fasting, the bible says in 1 Corinthians 7:5 *you should not defraud one another*. I am not saying you simply return to "business as usual" after an affair. That's not realistic or expected. It will take time to process all the different emotions you will feel - betrayal, anger, disbelief, pain, hurt... You must however communicate to your spouse that you will need time to process all your emotions.

So if he strays, seek God for the strength to forgive him. Forgiving your spouse is more for your benefit that his. The fact is, your forgiveness from the Lord is dependent on you forgiving your husband. (Matthew 6:14-15) It's a hard saying, but true. The good thing is that God is our refuge and strength and He can enable us to do what we think we cannot do. Earnestly seek God for His help. He is a rewarder of them that diligently seek Him!

87. Forgiveness – A Choice You Must Make ♥

Forgiveness is unlocking the door to set someone free and realizing you were the prisoner. Unknown

The matter of forgiveness is so important to the success of your marriage that it is worth repeating several times over. The bible is clear on the issue. If you want forgiveness, then you must forgive. We often pray the Lord's prayer so eloquently - daily even. A part of that prayer says '...*forgive us our sins as we forgive those who sin against us*'. In other words, to the extent that I forgive others, then Lord, forgive me.

Luke 6:37 says, *Forgive and you shall be forgiven.*

So, forgiveness is more for your benefit than for the offender. This principle sounds good. But it is by no means easy to embrace. When you are hurt, it is very difficult to see how forgiving the other person will benefit you.

We believe that forgiving the transgressor is letting them off the hook. But that's not so. It is really not about them, it's all about you and what you want from your God. As you are not yet perfect, you will make mistakes. You will sin against God and man. And you too will want forgiveness.

The fact is you can't afford for anything to block your communication with your God. The word of God says in Psalms 66:18, *If I regard iniquity in my heart, the Lord will not hear me*. Now that is a serious place to be. That is, to be in a position where irrespective of how many times you pray, how eloquently you pray, even how sincerely you pray, He will not hear you.

So yes, it's hard to forgive but it cost too much not to forgive. You must make the decision to forgive, repeat it to yourself daily, ask God to help you until you remember the offense without pain. That's when you know you have truly forgiven!

88. Pray About His Temptations

No one can be out of the reach of temptation unless he is dead. Robert Ingersoll

You are married to a human being. Humans make mistakes. Some make more than their fair share! You must be prepared to give your partner room to be human. I am not for one minute suggesting that you should accept your spouse making the same "mistakes" over and over again. He must be held accountable.

Genesis 2:18 called us to be helpmeets. One of the ways we can help our mate is to pray he will have the strength to overcome his temptations: whatever they are. And don't for one moment think that he should never be tempted.

If Satan tempted the Lord, who is your spouse to be exempted? The bible says in Luke 4:2 that Jesus was tempted forty days by the devil, and even after that, he continued to tempt him!

Remember Joseph and Potiphar's wife? The bible says *she spoke to him daily to lie with her*. (Genesis 39:10) Now that was serious pressure!

So my dear lady, it's not if your husband will be tempted; it's when! While you may not even be aware of what his temptations or struggles are, God knows. So ask the Lord to give him grace to overcome them. He may choose to share them with you or he may not. If he doesn't, leave him alone. Just pray, pray, pray without ceasing (1 Thessalonians.5:17) Note I didn't say nag, nag, nag without ceasing!

And when you pray, do not pray amiss. As the word of God says in 2 Peter 2:9, *The Lord knoweth how to deliver the godly out of temptations*. You must believe that God will deliver your spouse. Your duty is to pray and leave the results to the Lord.

89. Intuition Is Not Enough ♥
Extraordinary allegations require extraordinary evidence
Lance Armstrong

So you suspect that your husband is getting attached to another woman. You have a choice in your response. You could rant, rave and misbehave. You could seek to curse and confront the woman (something I'll never understand) or you could choose to go to God and earnestly ask Him to break up the suspected attraction.

Amidst all those options, please realize that suspicion or intuition is not evidence. It cannot go to court. Even if the Holy Spirit reveals it to you, remember the Holy Spirit cannot be taken to court. You therefore have to be careful how you pursue the matter when all you have is your intuition. This is said with the understanding that our intuition is one of the most basic instincts we have and is usually right. But I have also learned that a person will stoutly deny something they know to be true, once they are aware that you cannot prove it. If you have no hard evidence, you could make matters worse by making a big deal about it.

Accept the fact that your husband will be attracted to other women during the course of your marriage. This does not automatically mean that a 'relationship' will develop. These attractions are sometimes short lived. They are seasonal. So keep calm and engage the Lord through the season to put an end to any connection that may be developing.

Pray about the situation. Pray that the Holy Spirit warns your husband of possible imminent danger. Never underestimate the power of prayer. But what if the attraction develops into a relationship? Then you have a decision to make. (*See Letter 86 - If He Strays*).

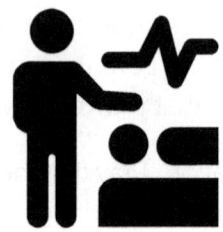

90. When Worse Comes 💙

You can't change your situation, the only thing you can change is how you choose to deal with it. Unknown

"I, (name), take you (name), to be my lawfully wedded (husband), to have and to hold from this day forward, for better or for worse, for richer, for poorer, in sickness and in health, to love and to cherish; from this day forward until death do us part."

That is the wedding vow you most likely adoringly recited as you stared in the love filled eyes of your partner. At that time, you may have repeated the words with absolutely no thought of their meaning. As far as you were concerned, this vow thing was just part of the wedding day that had to be done. No big deal. You were on cloud nine. You were happy. You were in love. Life was good. Praise be to God!

But then, it happened. Worse.... worse happened. Your worse can take any form. Loss of employment, sickness, infidelity, infertility, tragedy. And the list could go on and on. Very few people go through life without experiencing some form of worse. It is therefore not if, but when it happens.

While there is no one-size-fit-all solution to every situation, I'd like to suggest that you engage in active struggle to prevent the situation from overwhelming you. You must seek God's grace. Let Him know exactly how you feel. Cry to Him. Psalms 62 verse 8 invites you to *Pour out your heart before him.* God is a refuge for us. Ask Him for clear perspective. Ephesians 5:19 encourages us to *speak to ourselves in psalms and hymns and spiritual songs, to sing and make melody in our heart to the Lord.* You will not feel like it, but do it anyway. The feelings will come. You must encourage yourself. 1 Samuel 30:6 tells us that *David encouraged himself in the Lord.*

Someone once said that success in life is ten percent what happens to us and ninety percent how we react to it. Fortunately, we get to choose our reaction. It may feel unnatural to be happy and joyful in the midst of a bad situation, but we are not called to be natural. We must seek the help of the supernatural to empower us to respond in an unnatural way. We must fight to protect our joy. It's not escapism. It's recognising what we can control and what we cannot control. When we let go off what we cannot control and choose, (yes, there is the magic word - choose) to use our energy only in a positive manner, we will find ourselves experiencing more joy, irrespective of our circumstances.

Your "worse" will undoubtedly result in some stress to you but choose not to allow the circumstances to overwhelm you. "The greatest weapon against stress is our ability to choose one thought over another," so says William James. Phillipians 4:8 encourages us to choose our thoughts. It says, *Finally, brethren, whatsoever things are true, whatsoever things are honest, whatsoever things are just, whatsoever things are pure, whatsoever things are lovely, whatsoever things are of good report; if there be any virtue, and if there be any praise, think on these things.*

91. I Didn't Bargain For This ♥

Be miserable or motivate yourself. Whatever has to be done, it's always your choice. Wayne Dyer

So you are Christians; you and your husband. You attend church fairly regularly. But to be honest, you really have no connection with the people at church. Most times they drive you up a wall with their self-righteousness. As far as you are concerned, most of them are hypocrites because you know so many stories about them. But you still go. It is good to go to church but not to be too deeply involved. You are quite fine with your surface-level involvement in church.

So you are going on with your life and then it happens. Your husband tells you that he feels the call of God on his life and he is going into ministry. Or, he is called out as a pastor in the church. You are now catapulted into a high profile position; a position you did not bargain for. In addition, you can now hardly get any quality time with your husband because of the number of church engagements he has. Whether it is bible study, prayer meetings, counselling sessions, council meetings, visiting the sick… and the list goes on and on. You find yourself almost resenting the church.

Oh yes, resentment is a strong word. But if you search your heart, that's exactly what you may find there if you are honest. Be aware that resentment often leads to bitterness and bitterness robs you of your joy.

You have a choice. You can lead a miserable life or you can choose to think differently. In my view, you should not be a miserable Christian. Psalms 16:11 says, *In the presence of the Lord there is fullness of joy*. So you know what is causing your misery. You can't see yourself engaged in this new lifestyle of your husband. Or maybe it's because he is not there to help with the raising of the children. Whatever your reasons, justified as they are, you still have a choice. Live in misery or change how you think.

You must first decide to protect your joy. Let go of what you cannot control. You then look at what you can control. You can control your attitude. You could volunteer to be involved in some church activities where you can share time and space with him. If you are not so inclined, then you should support him as best as you can. When you decide to support him, say at a convention on a public holiday for example, it should not be obvious that you simply hate having to be at church at that time. It would be better if you were not there. You also have to be mindful of how your actions reflect on him. It certainly would not look good if he is at the convention preaching up a storm and you are in your bikini sunbathing at the beach!

The point I am making is, it makes no sense to live in misery. Choose to protect your joy. You will have to adjust your thinking and even some activities, but believe me, life is filled with unexpected changes, and while you may not have bargained for this situation, it is certainly not the worst that could happen.

You should consistently pray for your husband; pray that God will grant him wisdom to achieve a fair balance between his family life and church life. Every time you are tempted to be miserable about the situation, pray. Remember Proverbs 21:19 contends that *it's better to dwell in the wilderness, than with a contentious and angry woman*. So if you are contentious and angry (even if justifiably so) you may just be pushing your husband out in the 'wilderness' of more church activities!

92. Pray Him Into His Purpose ♥

We do not cease to pray for you, and to desire that ye might be filled with the knowledge of His will in all wisdom and spiritual understanding. Colossians 1:9

The blue print for marriages, which is the word of God, clearly sets out the respective roles for the husband and wives. Your husband is the head of the home, the priest and the protector of the family. I can see you rolling your eyes and saying, "Yeah, right!" You can only be justified in that attitude if you can truly say without reservation, that you are all that God intended you to be; that you are a finished product. You see, we are all work in progress. We are all at different stages of being made into the finished product. And no one gets to decide the stage at which the other should be. Ouch!

We may be tempted to think that once married, our spouse should automatically know what to do. And yes, you have told him many times, so he should know. Again, have you always done what you are told? And don't you sometimes just hate being told what to do. The point I'm making is, your role is to pray, sure you can suggest, but certainly not demand.

You may be surprised to know that many spiritual leaders, are not very spiritual at home, much to the frustration of their very spirit-filled wives! But you have weapons; prayer and a loving attitude. 1 Peter 3:1 advises that by your conduct they can be won.

It is a mistake to try and bully him into righteousness. Not even God does that. He says in Revelation 3:20, *Behold I stand at the door and knock, if any man hear my voice and open the door, I will come into him and sup with him and he with me.*

Your spouse must develop and grow into his purpose at his own pace. Your duty is to constantly pray him into that purpose.

93. Help Him Secure His Blessing ♥

Honour thy mother and thy father that thy days may be long upon the earth. Exodus 20:12

Some persons are very close to their parents while others are not. Irrespective of the quality of the relationship your partner has with his parents, it is not your place to help him widen a gap.

On the contrary, you should do everything in your power to ensure that he honours his parents. Exodus 20:12 instructs us to *honour our mother and father*. Unfortunately, the bible did not say "honour only the good mother and father." It did not make such a distinction. It therefore means that your husband's parents deserve honour.

Even if you are not fond of them, resist the temptation to say anything disparaging about them or to disrespect them You should also not encourage your spouse to disrespect his parents. So even if his parents do not act in a manner you or your husband think is deserving of respect, that's their business. Honour is still due.

If your relationship with them is not good, you should at least practice the adage, "If you can't say good, then shut your mouth!"

The bible promises a blessing to those who honour their parents. This should give you, as his helpmeet, the motivation to encourage your spouse to treat his parents well. Do all you can to help him secure his Exodus 12:20 blessing.

94. Time to Go ♥

Do not be a fool, why die before your time.
Ecclesiastes 7:17

I am a firm believer in the Lazarus principle. What is that? Lazarus was sick, he died, he was buried, he started to rot but Jesus said, "Come forth" and he did. Lazarus was brought back to life. The principle? Jesus can restore any relationship irrespective of the stage it's at. I have seen couples separate, even divorce and remarry and live happily ever after. Hence, my belief has modern evidence.

Having said all that, I do not think a woman should stay in an abusive relationship – whether verbal or physical abuse. The word of God in 1 Corinthians 13:4 tells us that *love suffereth long*; it did not say forever!

Abuse is never acceptable. Your spouse must know that a marriage is between two equal partners in the sight of God. If your spouse abuses you, he has lost respect for you, he does not value you. Your marriage is therefore in deep, deep trouble and needs help fast!

If your spouse refuses to get help then you must earnestly seek to leave. Be willing to accept that when you leave you may not initially have the same material things as you had before.

But it's better to be alive with your peace of mind though possessing fewer material things than to be dead or merely existing in a miserable, toxic environment with much material things. Many women feel trapped. They do not think that they can survive outside the marriage, especially if children are involved. Well remember, God is your source. There are many women with testimonies of how God saw them through after leaving an abusive relationship Sadly, there are also stories of other women who did not live to tell their stories!

You must firmly communicate to your spouse that while you appreciate the material things, (assuming that he is the provider) they cannot compensate for your misery. You must never forget that you are a valuable masterpiece of almighty God and no man has the right to abuse God's masterpiece. Ephesians 2:10 tells us that *we are His workmanship created in Christ Jesus.*

So if your spouse does not seek help and change his ways then, it's time to go!

95. From Your Mother-in-law ♥

Therefore, shall a man leave his father and his mother, and shall cleave unto his wife: and they shall be one flesh. Genesis 2:24

Welcome to the family. You can be assured that I will pose no problems, so please be at ease. I have no intention to interfere with your life. My son has chosen you as his wife and my only request, if you can allow me one, is to make him happy. As cliché as it might sound, that's what marriage is all about - i.e. developing the art of making the other person happy.

I have no intention to compete with you for my son's love or attention. I would never ask my son to choose between you and me (he would probably choose you anyway!)

Here are a few promises I am making to you:

- ♥ I promise to be warm and kind to you. I will never make you feel uncomfortable.

- ♥ I promise to respect you. And I do expect the same of you.

- ♥ I will not visit your home unannounced as I run the risk of interrupting "ministration."

- ♥ I will not criticise your style of doing things. I may make

- suggestions (even unsolicited ones!)
- ♥ I promise to listen to you if you need to talk.
- ♥ I will not search or roam about your home as if it were mine. I will respect your space.
- ♥ I will not compare your life with mine. You are not married to me.
- ♥ I will not take sides with my son just because he is my son.
- ♥ I will be fair to you at all times.
- ♥ I will not gossip about you.
- ♥ If I cannot say something good, I will shut my mouth!
- ♥ I will assist you if I'm able to do so but I would hope you would never take me for granted.
- ♥ I will not judge you based on any negative behaviour of your relatives. That would not be fair to you. You cannot control the behaviour of your relatives.

There are many horror stories about mothers-in-law. I do not intend to add to those stories. I will always pray for you and your marriage. You can count on that. We are now family, so I have a vested interest in the success of your marriage.

96. From Your Children ♥

Don't worry that children never listen to you; worry that they are always watching you. Robert Fulghum

Mother, we are so very grateful to be living with you and daddy. We are aware that we are very fortunate, as many children do not live with their fathers. In fact, many do not even know their fathers, so we recognise that we are privileged.

One of the best things you could give us is a happy home. A home where we not only feel loved but we see love demonstrated. We love to see when you and daddy show love to each other.

Now we know that you cannot control daddy's actions, but you certainly can control yours.

While we know that you will have disagreements. Can you stick to the issue; discuss the matters and not have a tracing match in the house? In fact, we would prefer if you had those discussions out of our earshot. We really do not think we need to hear.

Another thing mother, we know you love us dearly and you want to give us the best of everything including all your time. But the truth is, we believe that you should ensure that daddy gets his fair share of your time too. If he does not, then he may get miserable or he may not speak to you or to us. Tension will rise in the house and that makes us very uncomfortable. When there is tension in the house, we feel very insecure. So mother, we encourage you to strive to achieve balance.

You need to teach us that you and daddy need alone time. We believe that you should have a weekly date night; even if it is to go for a walk (in times when you have no money). Teach us to respect that time. We may not like it initially, but do not let up. Overtime, we will come to accept it. We know we can be demanding, and we will push your limit as far as you will allow us to. However, you are the adult; you determine the boundaries.

Mother, we want our home to be our happy place, so we encourage you to seek God's wisdom in building a loving relationship with daddy as we believe that's the foundation in helping us to have a happy home. Never forget that you are teaching us every day. The way you treat daddy teaches us how to treat our husbands when we get married and how we should expect to be treated by our wives.

97. From Your Best Friend ♥
A friend loveth at all times. Proverbs 17:17

My dear bestie, you know I love you. I also know that your heart's desire was to be married. Now that you are married, I am very happy for you. (Well to be honest, I am not always happy). I recognise that your status has changed and we certainly would not be able to spend all that time together as we used to.

I suggest that you schedule some time for us so we can keep our connection. Make sure however that your husband is in agreement. When I was at the wedding I heard the minister said, "What God has put together, let no man (or woman) put asunder." I would hate to know that I am the cause of any friction in your marriage.

I know we used to spend long hours on the phone chatting every evening. That certainly cannot continue if your husband is at home at that time. Because I love you, I will not allow you to be chatting away on the phone with me and your husband wants to spend some quality time with you.

I know I used to be all over your house as if I lived there. I accept that is a thing of the past. I know I can't be sprawling off in your matrimonial bed as I have a mind. In fact, I now know that I will have to be very careful when it comes to your bedroom. It would be very embarrassing for me if I came face to face with your husband walking around in his room in his birthday suit!

I know you will need a listening ear when things are not going to well. But try not to belittle your husband because when things return to the fine and dandy position, I will most likely still remember the bad things that you told me about him.

You need to know that I want the best for your marriage at all times. So I cannot promise to carry news to you that I know may cause problems in your marriage. But you can count on me to be always praying for the success of your marriage.

PS. I know that when we were single we promised that we would share all the details of our sex life when we got married. But I have thought about it and being a little older and wiser, I don't think that we should keep that promise. (Think about it). If your sex life is great, I may get jealous, and if it's bad I may lose respect for your husband.

98. From Your Pastor ♥

Wives submit yourselves unto your own husbands as unto the Lord. Ephesians 5:22

My dear Sister Right, I'm grateful for the privilege of being your Shepherd. It's my desire to guide you in your relationship with the Lord. I also wish to thank you for the high regard in which you hold me. I will try my best at all times to live up to that standard.

Even as I will encourage you to come to church every time the church doors are open, please know that if you adhere to that literally, you may not have a marriage, especially if your husband is unsaved. The truth is, your husband may hate me and the church if you are always at church and have little or no time for him.

Yes, I admire your faithfulness to the service of the Lord. Because of your faithfulness and zeal, I may even ask you to do many things in the church. Sometimes, it's hard to find those that are willing to serve. So I may get a little carried away in asking you to serve in several areas. Know that, if you over extend yourself, you may not be able to meet the needs of your husband. And when you are not meeting the needs of your husband, problems will arise in your marriage. So you cannot be at church every day of the week – every week of the year. You must make time to take care of the needs of your husband.

Remember 1 Corinthians 7:34 says, *The unmarried woman careth for the things of the Lord, that she may be holy both in body and in spirit: but she that is married careth for the things of the world, how she may please her husband*. It is important for you to remember this scripture. Try your best to please your husband as best and as often as you can.

Another thing, please do not compare your husband to me. And do not constantly tell him that, "Pastor says this" and "Pastor says that." Believe me, it will infuriate him. Ephesians 5:23 says *the husband is the head of the wife*; it didn't say the Pastor is!

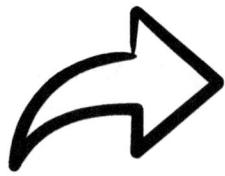

99. Going Forward ♥

Forgetting those things which are behind and reaching forth unto those things which are before. Philipians 3:13

I often speak with unhappy wives who have been married a long time and some for not so long. They opine that the level of toxicity in their marriage is such that they do not believe that there is any hope for a better marriage. They say while my advice is good in theory, it is difficult to implement in practice. They resign themselves to a loveless, confrontational relationship while secretly hoping that things could be different.

Well things can be different! And I am not a hopeless optimist, I am simply a believer. A believer in a God who caused the blind to see, the lame to walk; who raised rotting Lazarus from the dead and who call those things that are not as though they were! (Romans 4:17).

In my very short life (no pun intended) I have seen so many seemingly hopeless cases turn around that I am never ready to write off any situation.

In Nehemiah 1, when his brethren told him that the walls of Jerusalem were broken down, the word of God says Nehemiah wept, mourned, fasted and prayed. Then he decided that he would arise and build.

Likewise, you must first believe that the broken down walls of your marriage can be rebuilt. You should weep, mourn, fast and pray for your marriage until you believe! Then you seek God's guidance as to the right timing to use these two words: "Going forward!" Approach your partner and apologize for your failures which contributed to the breakdown in the marriage and promise a different course of action - going forward.

OK. You can exhale. I am sure you are saying, "And shouldn't he be doing the same thing?" And what if my sincerity is mocked and scorned? Well, it may very well be. But since you are not Lord Jesus and you do not hold the future in your hand, you really do not know how it will be received. Never under estimate the power of the Holy Ghost to change a situation.

And say you actually go through with the attempt and you are rebuffed, ask God for the grace to follow through with what you had committed to do. He will instruct you if and when to stop. By your chaste conduct you can win your husband. I have been looking and I cannot find any instruction in the word of God as to how long the chaste conduct should continue. I am inclined to think that we should ask God for the grace to make this chaste conduct our new way of life going forward.

100. Pray Without Ceasing ♥

To be a Christian without prayer, is no more possible than to be alive without breathing. Martin Luther

The word of God in 1 Thessalonians 5:17 says we are to *pray without ceasing*. I know we repeat this verse passionately, but I am not convinced that we even believe it is practical. I don't believe that this verse is saying that we should do nothing else in life, but be on our knees or on our stomachs praying day and night.

What I do believe however, is that we must be so connected with our God that praying is our second nature. We must reach out to God in every situation - when we are angry, when we are sad, when we feel hurt, when we feel betrayed, when we are disappointed, even when we are happy. The fact is, God is interested in all our emotions. He is our source. We would be less dependent on, or have fewer expectations of our spouses if we always remember that God is our source. The psalmist said in Psalms 62:5, *My soul, wait thou only upon God for my expectation is from Him*. Our expectation is from God. We should never forget that.

When we recognise and accept that, we will not get so angry or disappointed when our spouse disappoints us. And disappoint they will. It is not if it will happen, it's when it happens.

We must never forget that our spouses are imperfect human beings. It is not practical to expect them to always act perfectly. However when we are connected to God, when we are always in an attitude of prayer before Him, we will be more equipped to handle the issues that will arise with our spouse.

I therefore encourage you to stay connected to your source by praying without ceasing. It's amazing what prayer can do!

101. You Get To Choose ♥

The choices you make in life will make your life.
Michael Josephson

Someone once said that the most powerful tool we have each day is the power of choice. We get to choose our actions and reactions. In your marital relationship, you get to choose how you treat your husband. As a Christian wife, you have the manual, which is the word of God to guide you. The Lord said in Psalms 32:8 that He *will instruct you, teach you and counsel you.* I have tried to share the many lessons I have learned from my own relationship as well as those from other persons. I am confident, if applied, they will improve your relationship. However I am well aware that many of us are hearers and readers, but not doers of the word. Most times we justify our point of view even though we are well aware that our position will negatively affect our relationship.

One of the first quotes I read asked, "Why win an argument and lose a friend? It really got me thinking. I have never forgotten it since I read it. It has allowed me to temper my tone or overlook an offense.

So you get to choose if you will love, honour and respect your spouse whether you feel like it or you think he deserves it. You get to choose if you will say the first thing that comes to your mouth to your spouse or you will think before you speak. You get to choose. You get to choose if you will nag him about a matter or nag God about him. You get to choose. You get to choose how you will react to a potentially explosive situation and whether you will exercise self-control. You get to choose. You get to choose if you will forgive your spouse or thwart your own blessings through unforgiveness. You get to choose.

You get to choose if the imp that Satan has assigned to your marriage will succeed in destroying your marriage or he will be one of those who tremble when you awake. You get to choose. Many marriages are failing, not because the couples are incompatible, but because they fail to recognise the strategies of the enemy. Remember John 10:10 tells us that Satan's mission is *to kill, steal and destroy,* but Christ's mission is *to give us abundant life.* A Christian wife must be alert to the strategies of the enemy and resist him. The bible says when you *resist him, he will flee* (James 4:7).

I encourage you to commit your husband and your marriage to God on a daily basis - not when you remember, not when things are going wrong - but daily!

Your marriage was intended to be a beautiful relationship reflecting the relationship Christ has with His bride, which is the Church. The enemy has sought to destroy this wonderful institution, but he can only succeed if we allow him. I pray that you will not.

The word of God in 2 Peter 1:3 says, *According as His divine power hath given unto us all things that pertain unto life and godliness, through the knowledge of him...* In other words, we are equipped through the divine power of God to deal with the issues of life. I trust that you will choose to apply God's word to your life.

Conclusion: *You get to choose!*

Conclusion ♥

Despite the alarmingly high divorce rate, I still believe in marriages. I still believe that there are couples living their happily-ever-after. I still believe that irrespective of how sour your relationship is, it can be restored. There is nothing too hard for God (Jeremiah 32:27).

I decided to address the book to wives (although a number of the issues discussed apply to husbands as well) since I am a wife and can relate.

My hope is that wives will apply the contents of this book to their lives as I believe that if they do, they will enjoy not only their marriage but life in general.

Having discussed many principles in the book, I have pre-empted the question, 'Which ones are the most important?' And so, I have chosen the following 27, to coincide with the 27 years that I have enjoyed a very blessed marriage.

They are:

- ♥ Your marriage can be beautiful. You must believe this.
- ♥ There are persons enjoying their marriage. You can too.

- ❤ God is your source.

- ❤ Nagging will destroy your marriage.

- ❤ Constant criticism will prevent intimacy in your marriage. So focus on his positives.

- ❤ Always respect your spouse, irrespective of how you feel.

- ❤ Respect and validate yourself.

- ❤ Set boundaries for your marriage.

- ❤ Treat your spouse like a king whether or not he acts like one.

- ❤ Train your spouse how to treat you like a queen, but you must also act like one.

- ❤ Forgiveness is hard, but with God's grace you can do it.

- ❤ Think of something to be grateful for each day. You will be a happier person.

- ❤ Never compare your marriage with someone else's. You do not know all about their journey.

- ❤ Every day think of something that you like about your spouse.

- ❤ Everyday think of something that you like about yourself.

- ❤ Never take your spouse for granted.

- ♥ Pray for your spouse on a daily basis.
- ♥ Extend to your spouse the same courtesies you would to a highly respected person.
- ♥ Don't sweat the small stuff. He is not perfect and neither are you.
- ♥ Protect your joy. You should not allow anyone, not even your spouse to rob you of your joy.
- ♥ Laugh. Laugh often. Laugh heartily.
- ♥ Let go off what you cannot control.
- ♥ Sex is not just important; it is very important to your marriage.
- ♥ You must exercise great self- control, tolerance and patience or you will live in regret.
- ♥ Be deliberate about speaking his love language.
- ♥ Study him.
- ♥ You are responsible for your actions.

While I am well aware that the success of a marriage is dependent on both parties, I am also aware that the Christian wife who fears God, can greatly influence the fabric of that relationship. I do believe that with a little effort on a consistent basis, seemingly dry and dull marriages can be reignited and restored to a place where it can be the showpiece that God intended. So, Mrs. Right, do your part and do it right!

www.ingramcontent.com/pod-product-compliance
Lightning Source LLC
Chambersburg PA
CBHW071452040426
42444CB00008B/1304